C000243997

SURVIVING TOXIC LEADERSHIP WITH GRATEFULNESS

Dr. Margaret E. Gary

Dr. Margaret E. Gary

Copyright © 2020 Margaret E. Gary
All rights reserved. This book, or parts thereof, may not be
reproduced in any form without permission
ISBN: 9798587756441
Independently Published

Dedication

This book is dedicated first to my Lord and Savior, Jesus
Christ. Without your grace, mercy, unconditional love,
guidance, and protection, I am nothing.

Second, I dedicate this book to my husband, Malcolm and
children, Kendra, Roosevelt, Otavia, Kourtnee, Danyale,
Latoya, and Deontae. Each of you have permanently
enriched my quality of life. I am truly blessed to experience
your love, support, and encouragement. And, to my son-in-
law Travis, who actively listened and challenged me as I
shared research findings, keeping me encouraged and
focused.

Lastly, I dedicate this book to victims of leader toxicity
who consistently endure an overbearing weight of this
daunting experience. I pray this book employs toxic
leaders, and those who enable them, to understand and
acknowledge the errors of their ways and make the positive
changes necessary. Toxic leaders and those who enable
them must be held accountable, and victims must be given
the tools to become survivors.

Introduction

Four years ago, I found myself mired in a workplace

brimming with toxicity. I had been hired over a decade

before into a highly functioning company by owners who

were invested in the health and stamina of their employees.

The average tenure, when I began, was over ten years.

However, when the company changed hands, things quickly took a turn for the worse. We soon found ourselves working under a toxic leader whose approach to daily operations included dishonesty, arrogance, intimidation, and other demoralizing behaviors. Before our eyes, the workplace changed from a healthy space of collaboration to what suddenly felt like a prison. Some of us dodged our boss, hoping to avoid his most toxic behaviors, while others gave in and became complicit in his daily workplace abuse.

Working under a toxic leader, my coworkers and I experienced a range of physical, mental, and emotional struggles ranging from chronic sinus infections and irritable bowel syndrome to birthing complications, cancer, and even death. Our work environment was literally making us sick.

Since my resignation from the company, I have spoken with many other workers with similar stories. Like me, they had experienced extreme psychological and

5

physical symptoms, but felt unable to truly explain what they had been through. Often they had stayed in their position long after they realized it was having a negative effect on them, explaining away their boss's abusive behavior or justifying their decision to stay based on salary or perks.

As I listened to story after story, I realized that the previous literature on corporate responsibility and workplace abuse was unable to fully account for the experiences of working under toxic leaders. Excellent research had been done to explore workplace behaviors like bullying, harassment, sexism and racism, and other forms of harmful workplace behavior.[1] And yet, none of these frameworks seemed to fit. In each of these cases, I learned, employment law had evolved to clarify acceptable behavior. People who experienced these behaviors at work had possible legal recourse. The toxicity we had experienced, on the other hand, was difficult to articulate and often left employees wondering what we had done to

deserve the treatment we received.

But as I spoke with others, I quickly realized that

the problem did not begin and end with toxic leaders. Like

most toxic chemicals, leadership behaviors crept through

the entire system of the organization. It crept into our lives,

overcoming our workplace with a complex sludge of fear,

excuses, justifications, and self-blame. And what I began to

realize was that much of my frustration extended beyond

toxic leadership alone. I realized that I felt enormous

frustration with the complicity of other victims, particularly

those I'd been told had the power to stop workplace abuses:

Human Resources professionals.

Surviving Toxic Leadership with Gratefulness is the

result of my struggle to make sense of the experiences

others generously shared with me, as well as my own

experience surviving a toxic leader. But it is also more than

that. This book offers a systemic perspective on toxic

leadership, recognizing that the problem of a toxic workplace is never encapsulated in the leader alone. Rather, as I argue throughout the book, toxic leadership enacts a type of contagious trauma on those it touches. It can bring severe mental, physical, and emotional consequences to those who find themselves trapped in a toxic workplace, and these consequences often influence our reactions, creating complicity, ambivalence, apathy, and other behaviors that spread the harm of leadership throughout our workplaces and homes.

Since this problem is systemic, *Surviving Toxic Leadership with Gratefulness* advocates for a variety of solutions at both the corporate and individual levels. I argue that we must prevent toxic leaders from being hired or promoted, as well as work to rid companies of toxicity that already exists within the ranks of their employees. We must also look within ourselves to trace the ways toxic leadership has implicated us and caused us to act out of our own character and values. This process is not easy, and it requires that individuals find courage, perseverance, and the strength to heal. But while this work is not easy, it is ultimately beneficial to both the company and the individual.

Throughout the book, I speak to those who are either experiencing toxic leadership or who are observing it from the sidelines. With this audience in mind, I aim to achieve three interrelated goals. First, I share my own story. Those who have not experienced life under a toxic leader may not be aware of all the gory details. Therefore, while I have changed the names of those I worked with at my former company, I have included thorough descriptions of the events that unfolded leading to my resignation and, eventually, this research. Additionally, as someone who found great comfort in learning that I was not alone, I hope that my story can help others to see the patterns of abuse that tend to emerge in toxic leaders, and that this will provide some perspective and support for those working to free themselves from workplace toxicity.

Second, *Surviving Toxic Leadership with Gratefulness* offer research-based best practices for those who find the courage to advocate for change. By leaning on scholars of toxic leadership, as well as related social scientific research from experts in business, education, sociology, and other related fields. I take care to explain the various structures at work in promoting and supporting toxic leadership in everyday terms. This evidence can provide fodder for advocating changes in corporate structures and policy, particularly offering concrete documentation of the ways toxic leadership is harmful to companies in a variety of ways.

Finally, this book functions as a roadmap for improvement. It offers a plan for advancing your company's mission and vision through policies that eliminate leader toxicity. It also intervenes into the individual struggles victims and survivors of toxic

leadership often encounter, offering concrete ways of

healing and thriving after life under a toxic leader.

Together, the three aspects of this book can function

as tools in your toolkit, helping you first, to understand

what toxic leadership is and how it impacts individuals;

second, to advocate for change in your company and in

your own life; and third, to lay out a clear plan for ridding

your workplace and life of toxicity once and for all.

What is Toxic Leadership?

Before we can eradicate toxic leadership, we first

need to establish what toxic leadership is and how it may

be damaging your life and your company. The term *toxic*

leadership was coined by Rutgers University professor Dr.

Marcia Lynn Whicker in 1996, and it distilled her years of

research in a variety of organizations ranging from

businesses to churches. For Whicker, toxic leaders are

those who consistently display self-centered, dysfunctional,

11

and destructive characteristics. These leaders tend to engage in an array of unethical and socially irresponsible behaviors, including dishonesty, arrogance, and intimidation. Toxic leaders cause severe and enduring harm to everyone they come into contact with.

Early research on toxic leaders was parochial and focused mainly on bullying and similar dysfunctional traits.[2] Perhaps in response to the growing number of organizations suffering at the hand of toxic leaders, research later grew to examine the multiple layers that support and allow toxicity in the workplace to breed.[3] These layers include the follower's psychological need for a leader, structure of the organization, regulatory practices and policies of human resource management, and the subsequent organizational culture.[4] That is, leader toxicity will only flourish when a toxic leader is stimulated by a follower and an environment conducive to toxicity.

Toxic leaders are skilled at tapping into and

exploiting their followers' deep-seated psychological needs

and fears. This may be a learned behavior, with some

research suggesting that toxic leaders may themselves have

been exposed to a toxic environment.[5] Some toxic leaders

model their behavior after the patterns of abuse they have

experienced either in their families or in earlier workplace

situations. Alternatively, some research points to particular

psychological disorders, such as narcissism, that are often

characterized by manipulation and emotional abuse.[6] This

explains the tendency for toxic leaders to seek out

followers who are vulnerable to authoritarian leadership or

willing to go along with the leaders' personal prejudices

toward particular groups of people. Whatever the cause,

toxic leaders thrive on power, and spread their toxicity

through those who enable them.

Since toxic leaders are so dependent upon their

followers, toxic leadership is necessarily leaky. Toxic

leaders truly are the bad apple that spoils the bunch. One influential study led by North Carolina professor and media commentator Dr. Art Padilla solidified this approach, identifying what is appropriately termed the "toxic triangle."[7] Padilla's team identified three characteristics that work together to contribute to a destructive work environment: a toxic leader, a follower willing to support the leader, and an environment that enables leader toxicity to thrive. The interactions of these three components can make toxic leadership difficult to pin down. Some toxic leaders are unethical or evil, intentionally setting out to abuse and manipulate others. But some toxic leaders are simply incompetent managers, promoted into a role within a company that is particularly conducive to toxicity.

Toxic leadership not only varies in its intentions; it can also vary in appearance. For example, while the idea of a toxic leader may call to mind an overly demanding manager or a strong and reckless personality, these traits are not necessary for a leader to spread toxic behavior. As

United States Army Colonel George E. Reed points out,

many toxic leaders are soft spoken and come across as

genuinely invested in their organizations. He writes, "in the

end, it is not one specific behavior that deems one toxic; it

is the cumulative effect of de-motivational behavior on unit

morale and climate over time that tells the tale."[8] In other

words, it can be difficult to identify a toxic leader until the

damage has already been done.

Unfortunately, the damage that results from toxic

leadership can be immense. Research confirms that, if left

undetected, toxic leadership lowers morale, employee

retention, and productivity rates, spreading poisonous

behavior through the entire leadership system in the

organization. As a result, toxic leaders are expensive to

their organizations in ways that are often difficult to

calculate. They can also cause direct economic harm to an

organization. Since toxic leadership behaviors can create or contribute to a hostile work environment, they present a

legal threat to the organization through lawsuits and

settlements.

The Human in Human Resources

As I researched toxic leadership, I quickly realized

that the most fascinating accounts were emerging from

Human Resources personnel. These professionals had

found themselves in the middle of a nightmarish situation.

As the individual designated to solve issues of conflict in

the workplace, they became repositories for the many

stories of struggle from victims in their workplaces. They

had a bird's eye view of the toxic leaders they worked with.

At the same time, they found themselves entangled in a

system of toxic leadership, becoming victims themselves.

Of course, they had the option of reporting the leader to

corporate, realizing that those higher on the organizational

hierarchy were unlikely to take action against the leader.

They could also choose to allow the toxicity to continue,

trying where they could to support the leader's victims. Or

they could resign. Many of the professionals I spoke with

had experienced all three choices, and learned along the

way that none were ideal.

Since Human Resources managers experience such

a unique perspective, their stories are the heart of this book.

While plenty of excellent research exists reflecting the

quantitative costs of poor management, toxic and

otherwise, I chose to take a qualitative approach to toxic

leadership. As I spoke with the various Human Resources

professionals quoted in this book, I asked them to describe

and reflect upon their lived experiences, thoughts,

observations, and perceptions of toxic leadership. I

gathered information about the companies they worked in,

the attempts they made to solve the systemic problems of

toxicity in their workplace, and the solutions they would

recommend to others. Through our conversations, I aimed

to understand these professionals' stories on their own terms.

I began the research by carefully screening participants to ensure that everyone I interviewed met the criteria for the study. I interviewed each participant in person, recording and transcribing the interviews to ensure accuracy and allow for a careful comparative analysis. I then pored over the results searching for descriptions of toxic leadership. During this stage of research, I was particularly interested in commonalities between participants, and I aimed to find *exemplars*, or statements that serve as examples of commonly raised ideas, descriptions, or suggestions. These exemplars appear in this book as stories and quotes, but all represent at the perspective of more than one participant and some perspectives were universal.

In speaking with the Human Resources professionals in my study, it became clear that toxic leadership is an urgent problem. Over and over, interviewees told me that leader

toxicity was financially costly and that it reduced morale

and productivity. They shared stories of stressed-out

employees and leaders, and they recounted their startling

realizations about the increase in physical workplace

injuries once toxicity took hold. They told me about hours

of wasted time as they conducted and documented

investigations, performed mitigations, participated in

depositions, and signed on a parade of new employees once

the toxicity became clear and good workers began to

resign. As one participant shared,

> When you have a toxic leader, it is very disruptive
>
> to business. It affects all the employees of that
>
> leader's charge, as well as the other employees of
>
> the company. People talk, plain and simple. When
>
> you have a toxic leader, it creates a situation when
>
> employees look for comfort from others that they

feel will understand and that is often their peers.

This is very counterproductive for an organization. But beyond this, many of the participants I spoke with also reported experiencing the strain of leader toxicity themselves. They told me that they had experienced emotional and physical strain from their time working in toxic environments and reported overwhelming levels of stress. They regretted bringing anger and frustration home, fearing that their workplace toxicity had also impacted their spouses and children. Although they attempted to cope with the situation through activities like yoga and boxing, they grew increasingly aware that these activities were not enough to prevent the spread of toxicity into their personal lives. As a result, they often experienced shame at their inability to cope with workplace stress.

As I listened to their stories, I realized that toxic leadership is a true crisis, in that the very people we expect to manage the health of workers are themselves saddled with intense levels of stress. In general, the people we ask

to save us from leader toxicity feel impotent and ineffective

in doing so. Scholars of leadership have made clear the

crisis of cultivating leaders who are both authentic and self-

aware,[9] this has rarely been approached through the lens of

Human Resources. If we truly want to approach the

problems of contemporary leadership effectively, we must

do so not only by recruiting new leaders, but also by truly

enabling leadership watchdogs to do their job. This is the

case I make in *Surviving Toxic Leadership with*

Gratefulness.

Surviving Toxicity

As you read this book, I hope you will find a

connection between your own experiences and those that I

and my participants struggled with and ultimately survived.

If you are reading this as a person who is currently

experiencing toxicity in the workplace, or as someone who

has recently escaped a toxic leader, I hope that the stories in this book will be affirming and comforting. You are not alone. This book was inspired by my desire to share the knowledge that others have suffered under and emerged victorious from the same toxicity you are experiencing. If you are reading this as a person who is sympathetic to the problems of workplace toxicity and has the power to instigate change, either in your workplace or with a friend or family member who is victim to a toxic leader, these stories may be a useful reference. Often, victims of toxic leaders do not share all of the gory details about their experiences. If this has left you with any doubt that things are as bad as we say they are, the stories in this book will convince you that toxic leadership is incredibly harmful.

Individual experiences with toxic leaders are at the center of this book. Therefore, I have structured the remaining chapters to follow my own trajectory of struggling to find courage, persevering in the face of toxicity, working through feelings of reluctance, healing from the psychological abuse of a toxic leader, and finally

experiencing gratefulness at having escaped and survived

my toxic workplace. At each stage, I also include social

scientific research into the causes, structures, and impacts

of leader toxicity as well as the results of my own study of

toxic leadership and its survivors.

In the first chapter, *Courage,* I focus on the courage

that is fundamental to changing the situation of toxic

leadership at both the corporate and the individual level. At

the corporate level, courage is necessary to make change in

organizational structures that allow toxicity to thrive. For

individuals, courage is necessary to save ourselves and

others. The lack of courage in the face of toxic leadership is

prevalent, but unfortunately, hiding on the sidelines does

not actually protect us. Instead, those who lack courage

often find themselves the target of a toxic leader. This

chapter offers an overview of organizational structures and

23

Dr. Margaret E. Gary

encourages readers to stand up to toxic leadership in their
workplaces and lives.

Courage is a close cousin to *Perseverance,* and in
the second chapter, I argue that the strength to stand up to
toxic leadership must be nurtured through our communities.
Unfortunately, workplace communities are harmed by toxic
leaders, who often lack the emotional competency required
to encourage communal support, at times even intentionally
undermining efforts to build healthy relationships in the
workplace. We must therefore search for healthy
communities of support beyond our workplace to ensure
that we can persevere and survive in the face of workplace
toxicity. In this chapter, I also remind readers that we are
all responsible for each other's feelings of community
support, and I encourage intentionally building self-esteem
in ourselves and others.

We must also recognize that sometimes what
appears to be perseverance is actually *Reluctance.* Chapter

three focuses on the role of toxic followers, and points out

the problem of inventing "solutions" that actually enable

our own suffering. Drawing heavily from the experiences

of my participants as well as my own struggle under a toxic

leader, I highlight some of the unhealthy responses victims

may develop to toxic leaders. When these responses

rationalize toxicity, blame victims, or otherwise attempt to

fix workplace toxicity without holding toxic leaders

accountable, these responses are actually reluctance.

Reluctance is a central component of an ongoing toxic

leadership environment, and must be avoided, even if this

means removing ourselves from the situation.

Once we have escaped toxic leadership, whether by

removing ourselves or the toxic leader, we must then begin

the process of *Healing*. In many cases, survivors of toxic

leadership fail to realize the lasting trauma they have

experienced. By recognizing the trauma of toxic leadership

as trauma, we can begin to unpack the ways our suffering

has lingered within us. This allows us to process the traumatic experiences of toxic leaders and move through the stages of grief. Although some may wander "why all the fuss" over a job, it is crucial that victims of toxic leaders allow ourselves to grieve by giving ourselves the space to identify our experiences as trauma.

This book promises to help survivors of toxic leadership reach a point of *Gratefulness.* Of course, I don't mean to say that I am grateful for the abuse of a toxic workplace! Instead, in this chapter, I remind readers that it is important to be grateful for the lessons learned through our own and others' experiences with toxic leaders. Being grateful for this knowledge means using it to help others. I build a model in this chapter for understanding Human Resources as an *anti-toxin.* This model can allow companies to avoid the costly effects of toxic leaders by equipping their HR departments with the tools necessary to prevent toxic leadership.

SURVIVING TOXIC LEADERSHIP WITH GRATEFULNESS

It is crucial and urgent that we not only learn about toxic leadership, but *act* to end it. Toxic leaders and those who enable them must be held accountable, and victims must be given the tools to become survivors. I conclude this book by offering some concrete actions readers can take to support victims and make their own organizations more just. I survived toxic leadership with gratefulness, and I hope this book will help you to survive and to support a world where workplace toxicity is meant with immediate and appropriate consequences.

Chapter One

Courage

History will have to record that the greatest tragedy of this period of social transition was not the strident clamor of the bad people, but the appalling silence of the good people.

Dr. Martin Luther King Jr.

The year was 2008. I had been employed at my company for over a decade. I was confident, educated, strong, and accomplished. I had just finished earning my Bachelor's degree and was learning a bit about politics. An exciting young senator, Barack Obama, was running for president, and his energy was electric. I was excited to support Obama, and I was proud to be voting for the first African American President. Obama was a popular candidate, and I was comfortable talking about my choice. I was, however, also naïve. It had not even occurred to me that sharing my support for this up-and-coming political star could cause tensions in my workplace.

During this time, Nick, Catherine, and I often spent time together socially, as an extension of our workplace culture. One Thursday, as we were chatting over lunch, Catherine asked about my weekend plans.

"I actually signed up to help with the campaign, making phone calls for them."

"Which campaign?" she asked.

"The Obama campaign," I eagerly shared, expecting a lively conversation about my newfound political advocacy, but instead plowing head-on into a conversation that would change the course of my career for the next, harrowing, decade.

In response to my innocent comment about supporting Obama, I was taken through what felt like an hour-long history lesson. As Nick lectured me about politics, he asked a variety of increasingly aggressive political questions, obviously trying to trick me into siding with his Republican views. He accusingly questioned my views on abortion, and was incredulous about my positions on welfare.

As eager as I was to support Obama, and as deeply as I believed in his vision for our country, I simply did not have the political knowledge to answer his pointed questions, and even if I had, the abrupt shift in the mood of the conversation was unnerving. My inability to answer his questions only made him more furious. With twitching lips, he stated, "Voting is a privilege and people like you shouldn't be allowed to vote." As an African American woman, I was stunned. During the remainder of lunch and the very quiet ride back to the office, I examined, for clarity, the words he said, specifically the words "voting is a privilege" and "people like you." What gave him the right, I wondered, to explain to me, a woman of color, that voting is a privilege? And how could he so carelessly use the phrase "people like you," a phrase marked by clear racist undertones?

When we returned to the building, Catherine appeared in my office door. "I'm so sorry for asking that question," she said. "I had no idea it would lead to — to that! To you being drilled and attacked that way!" I knew she could see on my face how deeply offended I had been by Nick's behavior.

"You are way too strong to let them get to you," I silently told myself, hoping I could remain calm through this conversation with my Human Resources representative.

"I guess men are too emotional for politics," I joked, trying to lighten the mood.

Relieved to hear me making light of the situation, she jumped on board, and we both mocked the intensity of his reaction. We laughed, and she left. I moved forward, doing as I was expected. Everything went back to normal, at least as far as others in my office could tell.

I had viewed Human Resources as a sort of organizational police, and I deeply respected Catherine. The fact that she seemed to understand this incident as an interpersonal disagreement, rather than a workplace violation, sent me down a path of questioning and self-doubt. I saw the Human Resources manager as the police responsible for enforcing the organizational laws and policies. I viewed Catherine as protection. But even as my HR manager had knowledge of the abuse and toxicity, she lacked the courage to protect me.

The next morning, my boss came to my office and apologized, but in the same breath, he reopened the political conversation once again. This time, I was a bit more careful, and he responded more gently. He said, "I've watched you and your husband over the years, and I know that you believe in Republican values. You're financially responsible. You have a strong work ethic. You are homeowners. What is it that makes you believe you are Democrats?" he asked gently. "Is it that your parents were Democrats?"

I had found myself right back where we had begun. As I stared, he continued to explain that he, too, had come from a family of Democrats. "I followed my parents, too, when I was younger," he said, "but once I learned better, I changed party affiliations."

Dr. Margaret E. Gary

After what had happened the day before, I was afraid that if I failed to explain my reasoning for choosing the Democratic Party, eloquently and with sufficient support, I would face the same raised voice and twitching lips I had experienced the day before. Alternatively, I worried that if I allowed this conversation to carry on too long, I would lose my cool and let the "sister in me come out." So, although I can never recall my mother or father voting a day in their lives, I agreed, perhaps a bit robotically, "you're probably right. I likely chose this party because of my parents. They are Democrats." I hoped this would be enough to stave off any future political conversations with this man.

Unfortunately, the dam had been broken. In the upcoming weeks and months, it became clear to him that our last conversation had really been about appeasing him. He knew his attempt to control my political beliefs had been ineffective, and he was furious about it.

COURAGE

On November 4th 2008, I celebrated my vote. I arrived to work the next day exhausted, as I had not slept at all. But I was happy. I felt proud for America. I believed that America had moved one step closer to equality for all. One step closer to healing as a country. However, the years following this election, in that office and perhaps in the world, were brutal. Our public and private conversations changed. My previously glowing annual reviews saw a marked shift for the worse. Once, when I asked for a modest salary increase, Nick retorted that, "maybe you should tell your president to give you a raise," using my support of Barack Obama, now President of the United States, as an excuse for his hostile and aggressive behavior.

And yet, as furious as I was with Nick, my frustrations with him grew alongside my anger at Catherine. From Nick's initial attack that Thursday afternoon, she had not stood up for me, and even her apology that afternoon felt hollow, given her failure to correct his behavior in any way. A second incident unfolded, and then a third, and with each incident, it became clear that Catherine was not the ally I thought she was. My Human Resources representative was watching this unfold, and I was starting to ask why she wasn't protecting me. How could she stand by and watch Nick's behavior escalate to this level of hostility? Where was her courage?

In fact, Catherine's lack of action, her failure to actually do her job as the Human Resources Manager, is an important reminder that courage is not simply an abstract virtue. Rather, to talk about courage is to acknowledge a real and pervasive threat while simultaneously committing to do everything we can to dismantle the toxic power at the core of the issue. In that first conversation over lunch, Catherine did not realize her power to intervene. But even more egregiously, she allowed a pattern of abuse to develop and escalate, ignoring the power of her position to correct

Nick's toxic behavior in a way that could have benefitted me, as well as others in the company.

In this chapter, I address both the need for and lack of courage. When we fail to be courageous, we allow the dangers of toxic leadership to continue unabated, and as a result, we often experience feelings of shame and guilt, and we may even become collateral damage as the path of the toxic leader grows even more damaging. In this way, our fear is justified; it is based on the negative experiences we have come to expect from the toxic workplace, and from the clear potential of a toxic leader to harm everyone and everything in their environment. Being courageous is not always easy. But our failure to be courageous is detrimental to both victims and bystanders, including ourselves.

To truly realize the role of courage, we must first understand that the organizational structures that necessitate courage are often the same features that weaken our ability to feel courageous. To better grasp this distinction, let's explore the ways the twin roles of organization knowledge and organizational culture can work together to breed toxic leaders.

Organizations and Individuals

It is easy to imagine toxic leaders as lone wolves, singularly evil characters that terrorize everyone in an organization. However, it is crucial to keep in mind that toxic leadership is not only dependent upon organizational complicity; in fact, organizations that enable toxic leaders often help to encourage the damaging behaviors. These damaging behaviors, or *counterproductive work behaviors,* are those behaviors that harm or are intended to harm organizations and the people within those organizations. These work behaviors are central to toxic leaders, and they are often encouraged by issues of the organizational environment.

To understand the ways organizational culture can enable toxic leadership, even when that leadership is counterproductive to the organization itself, it can be helpful to think of any workplace in terms of its *organizational architecture.* When we imagine a beautiful, historic downtown building, our minds are often filled with things like elegant cornices, fluted columns, or the variegated tones of aged brick. But of course we know that historic buildings are only sustainable through their structural integrity; a balance of angles and counterweights, materials specially selected for their durability, and periodic structural maintenance. While organizations are not built of steel and stone, like buildings they are constructed from many hidden components that must be in balance if the organization is to function as a healthy, efficient entity.

Organizational architecture has many components, including the frameworks for decision-making by individuals and groups and the mechanisms of rewarding individuals for exemplary work, among other structure and systems that determine the day-to-day operations of any institution. In determining whether toxic leadership thrives in a particular organization, the most crucial component of organizational architecture is the system of security controls, particularly the role of *personnel selection.* Personnel selection consists of recruiting, selecting, hiring, and promoting employees based on performance. The aim of this security control is to identify individuals with relevant qualifications, experience, and personalities that are complementary to achieving the organization's short and long-term goals.

An important part of personnel selection is the use of pre-employment questionnaires. These tests allow organizations to evaluate an applicant's knowledge of the job, skills, cognitive and or physical ability, and their integrity and personality. It is these latter tests that can play a pivotal role in preventing toxic leadership, since measures of integrity and personality can help to determine whether an individual is likely to engage in counterproductive work behaviors. Integrity and personality tests are designed to measure candidates' attitude and opinions towards sabotage, workplace bullying, harassment, and aggression, among other counterproductive work behaviors central to the experience of toxicity in the workplace. But they can also reveal less obvious traits that might make individuals more likely to engage in the counterproductive work behaviors central to toxic leadership.

These personality tests can help to reveal both individual traits and combinations of personality indicators to help organizations protect themselves from toxicity. For example, "guilt proneness," an incredibly valuable trait for a leader, is the predisposition to experience negative feelings about personal wrongdoing. According to a 2013 study from Carnegie Mellon's Tepper School of Business, individuals who showed traits of guilt proneness were less likely to engage in counterproductive work behaviors.[10]

While this trait alone is valuable to employers, it is also important to remember that personality traits should not be considered individually, but in combination. As one 2011 study discovered, individual traits of consciousness, emotional stability, and agreeableness were less meaningful on their own than they were in pairs; those employees with high scores on two of these traits were less likely to engaged in counterproductive work behaviors than those who only scored highly on one trait.[11] As these studies demonstrate, there are many indicators of an individual's propensity toward toxic leadership that may be identified through strong hiring-based security controls.

Unfortunately, most toxic leaders are identified not through screening questionnaires or interviews, but through the harms they leave in their wake. For example, one Human Resources professional I spoke with shared that, for her, the most effective way to identify a toxic leader was through patterns of "excessive Workers' Compensation

Injuries." In fact, many of the professionals I interviewed discussed the prevalence of expensive problems like unusually high absenteeism, unusually larger numbers of employee complaints, and a noticeably increased rate of employee turnover. While best practices dictate the use of tools to identify toxic leaders before they cause harm to employees and the organization as a whole, often, organizations in my research "identified a toxic leader through the employees." The psychological, emotional, physical, and economic impacts of toxic leadership are so severe, Candice told me, that HR professionals can count on employees to "eventually talk when their leader is toxic. They will go to HR and express their concerns, or they will start talking with other employees."

With these clear harms in mind, it is easy to wonder why organizations continue to employ and promote toxic leaders. The answer is another component in organizational architecture: organizational culture. Organizational culture is a collection of learned knowledge that is transmitted both informally, through observing others in the workplace, and formally, through written policies and formal notices. Organizational behavior is all guided and filtered through the lens of organizational culture. When people discuss the idea of "fit" in decisions about hiring and promotion, they are really discussing whether the candidate's temperament and values match those of the organizational culture. However, since much of organizational culture is undocumented and informal, culture shifts over time depending on the behavior of employees and leaders. Therefore, a new employee or leader can radically change the organizational culture, for better or for worse, if their behaviors do not match the previous norms.

For example, many studies show a strong relationship between innovation and organizational culture. In fact, innovation plays such a pivotal role that it is vital to an organization's performance, and organizational culture is central to whether a business is able to innovate and thus survive new challenges.[12] Healthy organizations are open to, and encourage, changes in organizational culture that mirror shirts in broader society. On the other hand, organizations that stubbornly resist adaptation can often become a breeding ground for counterproductive work behaviors and toxic leadership. Since organizational culture often operates outside of our awareness, many organizations fail to recognize its importance.

Every organization's culture is unique. Still, there are certain structures of culture that can create a breeding ground for leadership toxicity. One particularly common structural factor is the choice by upper management to value apparent economic success over the health and safety of employees. This was the case in Serena's workplace. In her case, upper management so valued the toxic leader that they went beyond tolerating his behavior, and even to rewarded him for it. As she explained, the organization not only lacked a process for handling toxicity in leadership positions; upper management also saw this toxic leader as someone who could "get results." Unfortunately, as a result of being identified as a harmful manager, Serena's boss was actually promoted. This move spared his current employee's continued harm of his toxicity, but simultaneously rewarded him with an increased salary and a nice corner office.

For many in upper management, it makes sense to prioritize the bottom line. However, structuring an organization solely around the perception of current economic standing is a mistake. Most organizations believe that they must rely on management to achieve a competitive advantage,[13] and the decision of which leaders to invest in is often based on economic factors alone. In fact, many of the women I interviewed shared that their organizations ignored available personality assessments in hiring and promotion considerations, instead opting to base these decisions on "gut" feelings and analyses of visible economic factors. Missing from this equation is the vital link between organizational effectiveness and employee performance.[14] Leaders affect job productivity, satisfaction, turnover, and, ultimately, the performance of an organization. It also ignores the real, perhaps hidden, economic costs of toxic leadership that range from the expense of training new employees as a result of high turnover and the potential for lawsuits that stem from abusive workplace behavior. Research suggests that while most organizations understand the need to develop leaders, there is a deficiency in ensuring that leader development is linked to the organization's strategic process,[15] leading many organizations to view leadership through a false dichotomy of economic performance and employee mental health. As a result, toxic leaders are often tolerated under the false pretext of leadership development and investment, and when this happens, employee productivity is severely undercut.

Take, for example, Tasha's harrowing story of toxic leadership. Describing the environment as "degrading and unprofessional," Tasha recounted a series of escalating events in which the "president of the company would sit in senior management meetings and degrade, humiliate, and bully his senior leadership team." During her tenure at the company Tasha saw these behaviors chain out through exactly the type of organizational culture that breeds toxicity; her company's organizational architecture consisted of top-down toxicity with very few clear policies and procedures for dealing with company abuse, and because the ultimate value was placed on economic success for both the company and individuals within the company, employees were implicitly incentivized to support and encourage the toxic leader. As a result, Tasha witnessed common counterproductive work behaviors, such as gossip between employees, belittling, and blame. Additionally, because the toxic leadership flowed from the top down, she also saw more extreme behaviors, such as "managers ganging up on their subordinates to cover lies" and the firing of employees who attempted to reveal the toxic leader's harmful behaviors. Within this culture, employees learn that they must play along with the toxic leader or bear the brunt of his emotionally violent behavior.

In cases like these, an organizations' culture and spoken or unspoken policies are often a breeding ground for leadership toxicity. Representatives of an organization have a duty and role in advising and supporting victims of leader toxicity and mitigating the potential poison toxic leaders can cause. Employees want to feel secure in the workplace and in the organizations ability to intervene in the event of toxicity. However, if the behaviors are not taken seriously or if more focus is placed on the leader's ability to deliver and not the behaviors exhibited in the process, toxic leadership can fester and do harm to both employees and, paradoxically, the company's bottom line.

Collectively, leaders have a responsibility to define the organization's culture, establish desired behaviors, and demonstrate these behaviors themselves, thus acting as an example for members of the organization. This model is intuitive when we remember that a well-defined organizational architecture supports a healthy and thriving workplace culture, and that these components combine to encourage happy and productive employees. Ideally, the behaviors of both leaders and employees should benefit and not harm others and should not be egotistical, dysfunctional, nor destructive. Toxic leaders, on the other hand, negatively affect an organization's culture, contributing to reduced creativity, motivation and initiative, job dissatisfaction, and high turnover. To be truly effective, leaders must possess the skills and temperaments to maintain the health and safety of employees. Ideally, this should also include the ability to encourage all employees to contribute to leadership, either by taking on roles themselves or by commenting on the effectiveness of particular company processes.[16]

Why We Must Find Courage

Up until this point, I have focused this chapter on the meaning of toxic leadership at the organizational level. This level of understanding is crucial, because it allows us to take a step back and understand our experiences with toxic leaders from the perspective of a structure. While many people cannot be changed, most structures can, and it is crucial that toxic work environments are approached from a vantage of organizational architecture. It is also crucial that we recognize our own roles in this architecture.

Taking steps to remedy a toxic work environment requires a great deal of courage. I believe this courage must come from a place of empathy, for others as well as ourselves, driven by an understanding of the real psychological, emotional, and physical damage carried out by toxic leaders, and the ways this damage can prevent us from truly recognizing what is happening around us. As these patterns of behavior reveal, the structures that enable toxic leadership are truly sinister. Even as they require our courage, they drain us of our ability to see our own strength by seeping through the workplace and into our own homes. While this situation makes it very difficult to find the way forward, it also reveals why courage in the workplace is absolutely vital to surviving toxic leadership with gratefulness.

Toxic Leadership Damages Followers

While I have already discussed at length the ways toxic leadership damages employees, this point bears repeating here because it helps to illustrate the fluid nature of toxicity in workplace culture. Often the simplest and first recognition of toxic leadership comes from the direct followers of the toxic leader. A persistent theme in my conversations with Human Resources professionals was a sense of guilt and frustration as they witnessed good employees suffering through deficiencies in job performance, motivation, and health issues. Speaking from a place of human empathy in addition to the responsibility of the position of HR, these professionals described patterns of unfair punishments, self-centered attitudes, demanding tones, and blatant disrespect and disregard for others' needs. They shared that many good employees quit or were fired due to toxic leaders.

Understanding organizations as architectural allows us to realize that damage to followers is rarely, if ever, an issue for individual employees. Instead, damage to followers subsequently damages these employees' ability to work efficiently in team settings, an important component of company productivity and success. The HR professionals I spoke with not only described witnessing intense psychological damage, including issues of self-esteem and confidence that naturally impact our ability to work collaboratively. Many people I interviewed also described behaviors on the part of the toxic leader to actively dismantle teams. Often these leaders would use team situations to build their own power by pitting employees against each other, creating a competitive environment where open criticism and insults became the norm.

In one particularly glaring example, Serena described how a toxic leader "played members against each other." During team meetings, the leader would often share things that employees had told her in confidence, adding "her own spin." This strategy allowed the toxic leader to create division among team members, ensuring that the team would fight amongst themselves rather than turning against her leadership. Likewise, Maria described a toxic leader who intimidated team members through other employees; her boss would routinely tell one employee not to cooperate with requests from another employee, or send one worker to confront another about fabricated or exaggerated workplace conflicts. Rather than directly approaching employees, then, Maria's boss offloaded conflicts onto employees, thus manufacturing a toxic workplace, isolating workers from one another, and forcing them to rely on him alone. When confronted about his behavior, the leader feigned innocence, explaining that he would gladly speak with the employee and straighten things out. His insincerity was clear to the HR professional, and made clear to others as well when the leader was seen laughing about the incident with others.

Damaged Followers Damage the Organization

It is bad enough that employees suffer the harmful effects of toxic leaders. But it is also inevitable that the damage done to individual followers will have a disastrous impact on the organization as a whole. Human capital and the resulting labor costs are the largest of organizational operating expenses. A company's human resources or human capital is also imperative to competitive advantage. And yet, one of the most common issues raised by Human Resources professionals in my interviews was the issue of high turnover, a problem that carries with it not only an incredible economic cost,[17] but also a devastating cost to the health of organizational culture.

In the pattern of toxic leadership, employees become demotivated and ultimately unsatisfied with their job. Facing the types of follower damage I have highlighted in this chapter, many employees understandably chose to quit, rather than tolerate extensive suffering every day at their workplace. Others were fired or forced out of the company when upper management understood the toxic leader as more valuable than the reporting employee. In the most upsetting cases, some of the professionals I spoke with found themselves in the unfortunate role of terminating an employee whose performance had declined as a result of the toxic leader.

In these cases, employees' mental stability was so noticeably changed that the follower remained physically present at work while mentally "checked out." Some professionals I interviewed shared stories of employees who were once thought to be good employees. However, after experiencing leader toxicity they became disgruntled, dishonest, and even reckless with company property. In one case, an employee was reported by a co-worker for using the company printer after hours. When confronted about this behavior, the offending employee responded, "this is the least the company can give me for all the suffering I have to endure [from my boss]." Another participant reported numerous unemployment claims and lawsuits in which she had "no leg to stand on" as the HR professional and, therefore, the company had to settle.

Human Resources Professionals are the Collateral Damage

Finally, it is crucial for Human Resources professionals to speak out against toxic leadership, because they are often collateral damage. During my interviews, professional after professional shared stories of frustration, often feeling helpless or afraid to intervene as they witnessed the damage imposed on individuals and the organization. And yet, Human Resources professionals should be best positioned to mitigate leader toxicity. Why, then, do these well-meaning professionals fail to come forward and speak out on behalf of the employees they serve? The reason, I learned, is that HR professionals are often collateral damage, or the unintended targets, of leader toxicity.

Participants report emotional and physical remnants of their experiences with toxic leaders. Reports of overwhelming stress was common among participants because of their experience with toxic leaders. One participant described a physical ailment that directly related to the stress she was under after challenging a toxic leader. This experience caused her to leave the HR field altogether for several years until she had the "courage" to return.

Additionally, the effects of leader toxicity were reported to extend past the victims, to the victims' families, making the family collateral damage. Participants reported that they took anger and frustration home, which caused tension with their spouse and/or children. Several participants stated they took interest in activities like yoga and boxing, which calmed them before entering their homes. One participant described how her shame and feelings of incompetency lead to her inability to cope with what were previously considered normal stressors at both home and work. She ultimately had to seek counseling.

Standing Up, Speaking Out

It is no accident that the opening chapter of this book is titled, "Courage." Speaking out against injustice is understandably intimidating, anxiety-provoking, and even outright scary. And yet, as I have demonstrated in this chapter, failing to speak out has disastrous effects that ripple through followers, teams, organizations, and even our own homes.

Research suggests leaders, as individuals, have a significant impact on employee engagement, employees' mood, job performance, and psychological well-being. Toxic leaders compromise performance, health, and financial wellbeing. HR professionals' ability to influence outcomes is limited to their and the organization's level of competency, the way in which leadership regards the HR professional's role, and the HR professional's courage and tenacity to execute their responsibilities.

Over and over in my interviews, HR professionals recounted their care and empathy at the human costs of toxic leaders, and they shared their perception that their role as HR professionals was extremely important to an organization. Maintaining a safe workplace free of bullying and harassment was high on the list of responsibilities and priority. Yet most perceived they were limited in their ability to do so. The first step is having the courage to begin to do the work. In the next chapter, I argue that this work must begin with *perseverance.*

Chapter Two

Perseverance

Consider it pure joy, my brothers and sisters, whenever you face trials of many kinds, because you know that the testing of your faith produces perseverance. Let perseverance finish its work so that you may be mature and complete, not lacking anything … Blessed is the one who perseveres under trial because, having stood the test, that person will receive the crown of life that the Lord has promised to those who love him.

James 1: 2-4,12

Throughout my years working under Nick, the role of community was clear. In fact, it was even part of the physical layout of the building! Nick, Catherine, and I did not have offices directly next to one another. Rather, Nick was on one end of the building, I was in the middle, and Catherine was on the opposite end of the hallway. For either of them, it may have taken around two minutes to walk to my office. It's important to remember that we had been friends, and the three of us had built a strong community over the years. On a typical day, I would come to work at seven o'clock in the morning, and he was usually already at work. He would come in to chat around 7:15 most days and, particularly as his toxicity grew, he would stop back by my office around 4:30 in the afternoon as the day was wrapping up.

One morning, as he headed out from our morning chat and back to his office, he asked me to communicate with my team about a minor issue. "I hate to ask this, but could you please ask your team to be a bit more careful about how they process orders? I don't want to make a big deal of it or anything, but the little mistakes they always make are driving me nuts!"

"Sure, I'll email them this afternoon," I said, as he turned to leave my office, with a little chuckle to underscore how minor this was. As he turned to leave, he paused in the doorway. "Oh, and actually, Margaret?" he said, turning back to me, "I don't want your team to feel self-conscious. It's probably better if they don't know we've talked about it, you know?"

Feeling a little uncertain, but trusting that he had the best interests of my team in mind, I agreed not to mention him in the email.

"Thanks," he replied as he turned to go, "and just bcc me so I've got it for my files."

Readers who are savvy to the behaviors of toxic leaders will undoubtedly predict the sequence of events that followed that afternoon. Within 15 minutes of my email to the team, Nick replied to the team, making it clear that I had bcc'd him and insinuating that I had done so to undercut their collective reputation with the boss.

Of course, when he returned to my office for his 4:30 drop-in, he apologized profusely. "I'm so sorry," he said, shaking his head. "It just didn't even occur to me that your team would read it like that." I nodded, feeling increasingly uncomfortable with the games he was clearly playing with me and my team, who I liked and respected very much.

Shortly after the bcc incident, we hired a new employee, Rich, who was full of energy and drive. Rich was just a riot. Having him around brought a new sense of upbeat morale to the office, particularly because he loved to joke. One afternoon when work was a bit slower than usual, Rich had played a prank on me, putting an upside-down paper cup on my desk with a note that said, "Do not move!

Spider underneath!" I'm not afraid of spiders, and I knew right away that this was one of the new guy's signature office pranks.

Of course, Rich couldn't resist coming in to see whether his prank had worked, and around 4:15, he stopped by my office and plopped down in the chair nearest the door. "You are just too much," I said, rolling my eyes. It was clear the kid thought he was really clever. As we laughed about his creativity, Nick appeared in the doorway.

"Oh," he said, "I didn't mean to interrupt."

"No, no," I chuckled, "we were just joking around. Come on in!"

Glaring at Rich, Nick insisted, "No, absolutely not. I wouldn't want to break you two up. You seem like you're having such a great time."

I went home that evening thinking the incident had been strangely unsettling, and wondering what Nick thought he had walked in on. The next morning, it became clear. Rich had been written up for "horse play," and warned not to be caught doing anything similar in the future if he wanted to keep his job.

When I saw him in the break room that day, his entire aura had shifted. Despite my best attempts to reassure him, I could tell that Rich was not interested in hearing me out. "I don't want his damn chair anyway," he snapped, as he turned on his heel to leave. I soon discovered that Rich's comment about "his damn chair" was a reference to Nick's frequent presence in my office. Nick had caught Rich sitting in that chair the day before, and his retaliation had been swift.

Rich was not the only employee who had noticed Nick's ownership over my office furniture. Other women in the office would comment to me about how Nick seemed to like me, indicating that they believed I was receiving better treatment. I began to get the sense that others in the office saw Nick, Catherine, and I as co-conspirators, and this functionally isolated me from my coworkers and subordinates. Of course, I continued to vent to Catherine, believing that I could lean on our friendship to survive the toxicity that was rapidly spreading throughout our workplace environment.

I tell this story not to rehash the deleterious effects of toxic leadership in my life, but to emphasize the ease with which toxicity spread from one leader to infect an entire workplace unit. While various coworkers experienced Nick's toxic behavior differently, with some perhaps even interpreting Catherine and I as complicit or active participants in his counterproductive work behaviors, our leader's toxicity spread like a contagion through the entire office. Nick's behaviors impacted us all. But, importantly, they also took advantage of the very organization he was damaging; his particular strategies of control often leveraged the unit's organizational architecture, in the case of email practices and team-based vs hierarchical structures, and the company's organizational culture, turning Rich's innocent joking into fodder for workplace rumors and gossip. This process underscores the central role of community in the workplace. The networks of friends, coworkers, leaders, and followers means that toxic behavior often infects an entire organization through the veins of communication meant to promote transparency.

However, while community is affected by the emotional failures or abuses of toxic leadership, it can also be a solution, helping us to persevere and find our strength and courage in challenging situations. In this chapter, I aim to trace the community impacts of toxic leadership while also offering tips for using community to build perseverance and resilience. Perseverance and resilience are preparation tools that give power, and it is power that allows us to overcome roadblocks, obstacles, and adversity. When we set out to do a thing, we must know and be prepared for roadblocks, obstacles, and adversity, since these things are inevitable. Therefore, we as community members, in and out of the workplace, must take seriously our influence and responsibility, particularly in terms of the emotional and communal work of building self-esteem in ourselves and others.

It may be difficult to imagine the relationship between the contagious spread of toxicity through an organization and the purposeful uplifting of those in our communities. If we are to fully embrace our own role in spreading perseverance, we will have to understand what we are up against in an environment of toxic leadership. Let's begin by taking a look at the importance of emotional competencies in structuring workplace communities.

The Role of Emotional Competencies

In the previous chapter, I discussed the role organizations play in enabling and even encouraging toxic behavior. A toxic organizational culture, often marked by a top-down focus on visible economic structures, can help ensure that toxic leaders rise to the top of their company, where they can do the most damage. From here, their toxicity seeps down through the organizational architecture, damaging the people who allow the organization to function: the workers. By impacting workers, not only individually, but by weakening workplace relationships and communities, toxic leadership shifts the very foundation of organizational architecture.

But how is it possible for one person to do so much damage? The key to understanding the ripple effect of toxic leadership lies, paradoxically, in studying the techniques that allow *competent* leaders to function. These traits have been widely studied, but perhaps no research is more applicable to this particular context than "The Trojan Horse" of job analysis. Championed by a team of researchers representing Purdue University, Microsoft Corporation, Boeing Company and others, this "Trojan Horse," represents a model for understanding how *knowledge, skills, abilities, and other characteristics* (or *KSAOs)*, can help predict the competence of candidates for leadership positions.[18] While this research team suggests that individual KSAOs can be useful measures of some components of leadership, they urge executives to think of KSAOs as a constellation of interrelated traits that allow for not only the hard skills of the job, but additionally the emotional and interpersonal soft skills required of any effective leader. This combined set of skills necessary for healthy leadership is called a *competency model.*

Attributes of early leader competency models were technical in nature to include the leader's ability to plan, control, and evaluate the work of others. The basic skills of planning and evaluating are important, but when they are positioned as the only necessary traits of leaders, toxic leaders who produce economic growth in spite of the human and financial costs of their toxicity slip through the cracks. In fact, one research team refers to *competency modeling* as a "Trojan Horse," highlighting the ways competency modeling can often pass muster with executive leadership where other screening questionnaires were ignored or dismissed in favor of visible economic productivity.

Whereas the dependence on visible economic productivity often encourage the development of toxic leadership, competency modeling that goes beyond the basic ability to "plan control and evaluate" can ensure that a leader is willing and able to support a healthy organizational culture. This require crucial skills in motivating and inspiring others,[19] the so-called "soft skills" that allow a leader to create a culture rooted in the company's values, vision, and mission.[20] A competency model focused on preventing toxic leadership must centralize the trait of Emotional Intelligence, a trait that has been shown to have a significant impact on employee engagement, mood, job performance, and psychological well-being.

Sometimes called Emotional Intelligence (or EI), EQ is a measure of personal attributes critical for managing emotions. Broken down into its component parts, EQ consists of self-awareness, self-regulation-motivation, empathy, and social skills.[21] Self-awareness: recognizing your emotions, what makes you happy, mad, sad. Knowing your strengths and weaknesses. Self-regulation: controlling your emotions, reactions, and behaviors as stimulants are presented. Self-motivation: being motivated by internal factors (passion, achieving personal goals) verses external rewards (recognition, money). Empathy: being able to understand and respond appropriately to others' feelings. Social Skills: being able to connect with people and build healthy relationships. Increasingly, management scholars and consultants realize how important it is for managers and leaders to understand and manage their emotions.

Together, these components form a leader's EQ, and the higher the competency, the more skilled a leader is at responding to and working with their followers. Since confidence is rooted in the attributes of EQ, leaders with higher EQ tend to appear more competent, a motivational trait that is also aided by the strong communication skills possessed by leaders with high EQs.[22] In fact, emotional intelligence is such a powerful predictor of leadership that one study from the University of Würsberg discovered that an emotionally intelligent leader can synchronize behavior of everyone in a firm, spreading the positive features of motivation, empathy, self-awareness, and other aspects of EQ throughout the organization as a "mood contagion."[23]

However, this "mood contagion" effect is not limited to those with good intentions or supportive behaviors. In fact, some research suggests a relationship between poor ethical behavior and low EQ skills.[24] This finding is particularly troubling, given that an astonishing number of leaders lack EQ skills,[25] and this lack of self-awareness and empathy can result in toxic leaders who do not recognize their own toxicity. For example, toxic leaders who lack social skills, a central component of EQ, may view their counterproductive work behaviors as socially normal. Often this sense of normalcy combines with low levels of empathy and self-awareness to produce toxic leaders who are unable to comprehend the damaging effects their behaviors have on others. In some cases, toxic leaders have themselves been exposed to a toxic environment, leading them to believe that even their most destructive behaviors are "for the good of the company,"[26] or simply a necessarily pain of productivity. And, of course, leaders who have not been properly trained in their role, and who are already prone to low-EQ behaviors, may overcompensate, resulting in toxic counterproductive work behaviors.

Toxic leaders consistently display self-centered, dysfunctional, and destructive characteristics. As a result of their emotional incompetence's, these leaders are prone to dishonesty and arrogance,[27] and they often exhibit counterproductive work behaviors that result in their followers feeling intimidated, demoralized, or undermined. Bad ethics and behavior could be motivated by an individual's attempt to satisfy personal needs, the leader's personal prejudices, or an attempt to increase his or her personal status or power.[28] As Walden University doctoral researcher Sabrina Michele Maxwell writes, some individuals are "born with a natural tendency toward narcissism, authoritarian and abusive behaviors [and] attitudes of self-promotion."[29] In these cases, it can be difficult for those untrained or unexperienced in dealing with narcissistic and malignant narcissistic personality disorders to recognize the ways they are being manipulated. Toxic leaders of this kind are skilled at recognizing and exploiting their individual follower's deep-seated psychological needs and fears.

All followers are part of larger organizations, connected to one another through organizational architecture and informal cultural roles. Therefore, the impacts of toxic leadership are not limited to the individual. In one of the most comprehensive studies of toxic leadership to date, California State-San Bernardino researcher Kathie L. Pelletier surveyed 215 employees, 189 of whom had experienced toxic leadership directly. Pelletier found that toxic leaders very often attacked employees at an emotional level, and that these emotional attacks tended to destabilize workers' sense of belonging and community support. For example, these leaders often attacked participants self-esteem, used deceptive tactics, or even threatened them psychologically or physically. As harmful as these behaviors are, the serious and enduring impacts occurred as these emotional contagious rippled through the architecture of the team or organization, often through the toxic leader socially excluding individuals, causing discord amongst team members, and promoting inequalities. These counterproductive work behaviors, then, do not only harm individual workers, but do serious and enduring harm to organizations at the cultural and architectural levels.

The contagious nature of toxic leadership is not isolated to particular teams or units within a larger organizational architecture; just as unidentified mold can spread throughout the walls of a building, stealthily spreading toxicity throughout an entire space, toxic leadership often spreads throughout the entire organization.[30] As the old adage goes, one bad apple spoils the bunch. Writing in the *Harvard Business Review,* Daniel Goleman, Richard Boyatzis, and Annie McKee note:

> We found that of all the elements affecting bottom-line performance, the importance of the leader's

mood and its attendant behaviors are most surprising. That powerful pair set off a chain reaction: The leader's mood and behaviors drive the moods and behaviors of everyone else. A cranky and ruthless boss creates a toxic organization filled with negative underachievers who ignore opportunities; an inspirational, inclusive leader spawns acolytes for whom any challenge is surmountable. The final link in the chain is performance: profit or loss.[31]

As key constitutes of ethical stewardship in an organization, toxic leaders set the tone for the entire business infrastructure. Of course, doing so requires so-called hard skills including planning, controlling, and evaluating projects and general productivity. However, given that leaders are also a vital link between organizational effectiveness and employee performance, they also contribute to organizations on the level of emotional well-being. Their ability to positively impact job productivity, satisfaction, turnover, and, ultimately the performance of organization[32] is therefore determined as much by their "soft skills," with their emotional competencies and EQ playing a particularly large role in their potential effectiveness.

Community-Based Resilience

Unfortunately, many executives fail to identify or reject potential leaders who lack emotional intelligence. When this happens, and toxic leadership develops or continues as a result, the responsibility for persevering in spite of an emotionally abusive environment falls on the employees. Employees of toxic leaders must develop mechanisms for coping, and often these begin with our lives outside the workplace. Leadership expert Professor Jean Lipman-Blumen reminds us that humans have a basic psychological need for authority, order, security and belonging; they fear ostracism, powerlessness, and uncertainty.[33] These needs are often exploited by toxic leaders, and used to manipulate their followers. Importantly, though, we can ensure that our emotional needs are met outside the workplace, thus allowing us to build perseverance to survive our toxic workplace and helping us to avoid the most dangerous pitfalls of the spread of toxic leadership.

A few years ago, my minister, an avid weightlifter, opened the sermon by lifting his arms and flexing his muscles to the congregation.

"Look at these muscles," he bragged, with a contagious grin spreading across his face. "Now these muscles allow me to lift things that some of y'all can't. These muscles allow me to achieve goals some of y'all can't."

Still smiling, he asked, "How do you think I got these muscles?".

Many laughed and responded, "working out," "the gym," "weights."

However, a fellow weightlifter in the congregation responded, "by enduring pain."

The minister said, "That's right. Enduring pain, persevering. You have to experience pain to get muscle. There is no way around it. In fact, nobody with muscles can tell me they didn't persevere through pain to get them. Nobody." Turning serious, he continued, "People, let me ask you something else. Do you think getting spiritual muscle is any different?"

While the sermon served as a reminder to the congregation that persecution is inevitable, it also forced me to reflect on the persecution in my life. Being raised by a drug addicted mother and an alcoholic stepfather certainly gave me an early "workout," allowing me to build spiritual muscle through my persistence in a bad situation. While listening to the sermon, I started to rejoice. I found myself feeling grateful to God for always being with me. I reflected on the fact that God has prepared my path, building me up, so that I may get through life's next challenge.

This sermon was influential to me truly connecting the power of faith and spiritual muscle to all aspects of my life. Before this moment, I had rarely evaluated the constant interaction of my spiritual muscle, my work obstacles, and my perseverance. My minister's words helped me to realize that these components are all deeply intertwined.

In my pastors' example, obstacles and interference came in the form of pain. This pain is part of the process and therefore unavoidable. Throughout the sermon, he continuously referenced God's word as his motivator in overcoming pain. I chuckled, because I suspected the "atta boys," complements, and stares of enjoyment from his gym community equally influenced his ability to persevere. We must not discount our purpose as a community in the process of building muscle or strength in others.

Obstacles, interference, and adversity are common experiences in the journey of achieving goals and fulfilling purpose. Perseverance is the continued persistence in achieving goals and fulfilling purpose, even in the face of these difficulties and delays. Most of us learn how to respond to these experiences through trial and error. That is, perseverance is typically not a part of a school curriculum, nor is it included in workplace training. Yet, success in every aspect of life requires it.

Working in a toxic workplace can help to build our perseverance, but importantly, the perseverance we build earlier in life can also help us to conquer toxic leadership. We need our communities to help us to construct our self-esteem and self-worth, thus preparing us for the challenges of the workplace. But our role in a community is not only in building up our own spiritual muscle; our purpose as a community is also to build strength in others. Self-esteem and self-worth are antecedents of perseverance. I can remember the elders in my community proclaiming "Child, you can be anything you want to be, have anything you want to have, because you are a child of God." They would encourage me by saying, "God created you for greatness." My favorite proclamation, specifically over my life, is from a neighbor in my community. Beginning when I was only ten years old, and continuing to this day, Mr. Welcome greets me saying, "There's our businesswoman." As a young girl and then as a young woman, these words nurtured my vision and goal setting. They served as a blueprint for what my community expected of me. They gave me hope, boosted my self-esteem, and provided the confidence needed to build spiritual muscle. More importantly, his continuation of this statement, throughout my adulthood, held me accountable for the outcome of my life.

PERSEVERANCE

I am especially grateful to Mr. Welcome, who didn't just say I can, but who said I was!! You see, everyone in a community is responsible for giving the hope and self-esteem needed to build spiritual muscle, the key to perseverance. While this encouragement should start during childhood, don't discount what the work community can provide. Much of my work community made similar contribution to my perseverance.

Resilience differs from perseverance in that it offers long-term endurance. But it is often difficult to differentiate between resilience and perseverance in a toxic community. Those who find themselves in situations with toxic leaders will often unconsciously seek out ways to develop resilience. For example, many of the Human Resources personnel I spoke with described seeking social support from colleagues at work. This practice, called "debriefing," can offer a path toward building resilience when it is used in a healthy and purposeful way. Unfortunately, debriefing can sometimes devolve into gossip, which may unintentionally create factions between employees and thereby undermine the possibility of one potential resilience-building community. I will discuss this problem further in the next chapter, pointing out more problems with things like gossip and cliques and why they should be avoided, as they often escalate situations by contributing to the development of toxic followers.

On the other hand, some of the participants I spoke with strategically used debriefing in a way that allowed them to begin building resilience. Marquis, for example, realized that many employees were coming to him to debrief after increasingly aggressive encounters with their regional manager. Rather than simply listen to them and give advice, he began to firmly and clearly communicate with employees that the toxic leader's behavior was inappropriate, and that it should not be tolerated. Marquis used the series of debriefings to build a consistent set of reports to corporate. Unfortunately, corporate Human Resources departments, in my and my research participants experience, fall short in actually dealing with toxic leaders. Still, by reporting each and every incident, Marquis helped to send a message to the employees he worked with that the toxic behavior was wrong, that this behavior was not their fault, and that they had value beyond this particular workplace. This approach can help build resilience in employees, allowing them to do what is right for their own mental and physical health, regardless of the actions of a corporate office.

Marquis was not alone in his approach. In fact, many of the male participants in my study displayed similar kinds of strength in their encounters within the toxic workplace. While acknowledging that he, too, was a victim, Kevin described his toxic workplace as a space where he was uniquely equipped to protect and defend others. As the building's Human Resources manager, and we might infer as a result of the way he saw his own masculine identity

playing out within an emotionally dangerous space, Kevin

often chose to directly intervene. In one shocking story, he

recounted observing an encounter between a toxic boss and

the company's security personnel. Taking care to put safety

first, the guards continued to load their weapons when their

boss entered the room. However, this toxic leader felt that

they should have stopped everything to acknowledge his

presence.

The boss "went ballistic," passive aggressively

bemoaning the situation and making everyone

uncomfortable. Rather than allow the situation to proceed,

Kevin said, he asked the toxic leader to step outside the

room to talk. Then he, "immediately took ownership of the

issue and explained that I did not know the proper

protocol." By taking ownership of the "mistake," Kevin

was able to protect his fellow employees while calmly

explaining that "it was unsafe for the security personnel to stop in the middle of loading live rounds to acknowledge his presence." Because Kevin felt comfortable in his own skin and confident in his value in and out of the workplace, he felt empowered to speak up.

Of course, while it is crucial that we help build resilience in others, it is also important that we participate in communities that give us strength and a sense of personal value outside the workplace. Marquis and Kevin helped to save others, but it is just as important that they build communities of support to help cultivate their own sense of self-value. I saw the clear results of having a strong sense of self-value and self-efficacy in Devon, who told me clearly and without hesitation, "listen, you don't let the toxicity get out of hand." He advised that Human Resources personnel and other workers should

> stand up to them instantly. I believe in being open. Let them know you see them. Require them to accept the help you're offering or leave. This must

be done before the leader hurts people. I've had to do this with several toxic leaders, even some who were toxic toward me. This method has always worked for me.

It is important to point out that the ability to diffuse a situation directly and clearly in the way that "always worked for" Kevin can be an extension of identity. Approaches that are successful for white men may send very different messages when delivered by Black men and women, often unfairly stereotyped as "angry" or "aggressive," even when we go out of our way to be conciliatory. It is no coincidence that the men in my study were much more likely to face toxic leadership in a directly assertive way, given the differences in socialization between men and women and the ways factors like gender, race, and sexuality impact interpretations of workplace behavior and attitude.

However, this does not mean that only white men are capable of building resilience like Kevin's. Rather, it means that we all must recognize the particular obstacles we must overcome as individuals. Some of these may be related to issues of race or gender, as long as society continues to give us an unequal playing ground. Other factors may be more personal, including things like a generally low self-esteem or a conflict avoidant personality. Recognizing the barriers we face can help us to name our experiences and develop strategies for facing them and emerging healthier and more resilient than ever. It is for this reason that I recommend finding a space beyond the workplace to build up your sense of resilience. A strong community that truly sees and understands the layers of what you're going through, whether in your church, a group of friends, or a therapy circle, it is crucial to the ability to build resilience and practice that strength in your toxic workplace.

Resilience is "a mental ability to recover from or adjust easily to misfortune or change." Nelson Mandela said, "do not judge me by my success; judge me by how many times I fell down and got back up again." The continued act of getting back up is a true measure of resilience, but the ability to do so is rarely developed alone. I am grateful to all who gave me the tools needed to persevere or outlast, not avoid, opposition and, to others who participated in my process of getting back up. In other words, I am grateful to the community that helped me build resilience. We don't have to do this on our own. We can lean on our families, our friends, and our communities to help us develop the tools we need to stand up to toxic leadership.

There are many things in a workplace that we cannot control. When we build up our own resilience, we allow ourselves to understand this, name it, and make the best decisions for ourselves. We take control of the only thing we truly can: our own lives.

When You've Just Got to Hold On

As Lipman-Blumen notes, we all have a basic set of psychological needs. If we are not able to fulfill these needs, or if our emotional state is compromised by workplace toxicity, we become particularly susceptible to the narcissistic and emotionally unintelligent strategies of toxic leadership. Since we all want to feel a sense of belonging and support at work, it is easy to get drawn in by toxic leaders, looking for the psychological support that they cannot and will not provide for us. Toxic leaders, research shows, often possess a low level of emotional intelligence, and may even display narcissistic tendencies. It is a mistake to seek out community in their presence, because their toxic traits often travel throughout our workplaces like a contagion. When this happens, the responsibility for persevering in spite of an emotionally abusive environment falls on the employees. One solution is to develop *spiritual muscle,* particularly through leaning on our communities of support.

As I have discussed in this chapter, perseverance is a necessary component to surviving toxic leadership with gratefulness. Still, perseverance is not enough. We must also recognize the propensity for toxic leadership to undermine our best efforts to find and build community. In the following chapter, I identify a primary way toxic leaders subvert our attempts to push back against their abuse: *reluctance.*

Chapter Three

Reluctance

Ah, when to the heart of man was it ever less than a treason to go with the drift of things, to yield with a grace to reason, and bow and accept the end of a love or a season?

Robert Frost

By 2016, I had endured nearly a decade of passive aggressive, and occasionally direct aggressive, treatment from my boss. So when Nick strode into my office one afternoon and pushed the door closed behind him, I was immediately apprehensive.

"Here's the thing, Margaret," he said, feigning a calmness belied by the aggressive energy bubbling beneath the surface. "I've been thinking about what you said yesterday, and I'm sorry, but I just cannot let this go..."

Dumbfounded by his insistence on rehashing a casual conversation from the previous day and glancing anxiously to the closed door behind him, all I could do was stare blankly.

"I just ..." he sputtered, "how dare you argue with me about something I care so passionately about, when you obviously haven't taken the time to really understand. This is exactly the problem with people like you..." As he continued to explain his opposing opinion, his lips began to twitch in anger, and I became increasingly concerned for my safety. From that point in the conversation, I remember very little of what he said. I watched in horror as his fury grew more and more physical, and when he escalated from forceful finger pointing to charging toward my desk, I tried desperately to retract and explain my previous statement. Nick towered over me with a rage beyond anything I'd seen in the previous 10 years of his toxic behavior, with a red face, twitching lips, and the frantic gesturing of a man intent on hurting me.

Tears rolled down my face, and, shaking, I braced myself for a physical attack. Something about my posture must have signaled to Nick that he had gone too far. Suddenly, he began backing away, looking around the room as if disoriented by the office itself.

"Margaret, I—" he started, and I struggled to catch my breath as adrenaline pumped through my body. "I didn't mean to … I was just …" Somewhere in his stammering, I think he apologized. For a few moments, we just stared at each other. Then, he turned to leave. Just as his hand touched the doorknob, he looked back at me and said, with the careful composure of someone well-versed in emotional manipulation, "I always viewed you as stronger than this."

The instant I heard the latch click shut behind him, I ran to the door and locked it behind him. Then, I picked up the phone and called Catherine. She was in my office in record time, and we both sat, horrified, watching the door and planning our next steps.

You may be assuming that it was Catherine, as our local Human Resources manager, who eventually contacted the corporate office. You would be wrong. Tired of waiting, I finally emailed them with an account of the incident, on which I cc'd Catherine. At that point, she finally filed an official report. That email was not easy to send. I hadn't had much contact with corporate Human

Resources, and I had no idea whether they would be sympathetic to the situation or, like Catherine, reluctant to rock the boat. Still, I knew she could not fix this. In that email, and my subsequent communications with corporate Human Resources, I spelled out everything that had happened over the past decade. This was a clear pattern of toxicity, I told them, and Catherine had known all along.

Days later, I sat in my office with the Vice President of Human Resources for North America.

"First of all, Margaret, we all want you to know that we are so sorry this happened." I nodded, naïvely believing that justice might be served. "We've spoken with Nick, and he has acknowledged many of the incidents you reported. Thank you for maintaining such thorough documentation. That's unusual, and we all believe it has really helped us to fairly evaluate the situation."

Feeling cautiously optimistic and finally at ease again in my office, I breathed a sigh of relief. Nick would finally face some consequences, and maybe our workplace could heal. "Thank you so much," I said. "I'm so relieved."

"This is why we were able to take action. Nick will be enrolled in a course of anger management training, and I've gotten approval to cover the costs for any counseling you'd like to receive," she said. "We really think this will do so much to improve the organizational culture, so we appreciate your openness about the whole situation."

I can't be sure that my mouth didn't drop open at this. Nick had already attended anger management courses for separate incidents, even before he nearly physically attacked me the week before. Shocked, but wanting to remain professional with the corporate representative, I nodded silently.

"So with Nick's behavior taken care of," she continued, "the thing we need to know is whether you'd like to resign. I worked hard to clear this with corporate, and I'm excited to be able to offer you a very generous severance package."

"Why should I resign?" I blurted out. "I like my job! I want to be here. I've been here for nearly twenty years. I just want my boss to stop abusing me!"

It was at this point that the veil lifted from my eyes. This woman had come from New York to solve a problem, but it was not the problem of Nick's abuse. It was the problem of me complaining about his toxicity. They recognized the hostility of the workplace, but they were reluctant to discipline a high-earning CEO. They chose, instead, to continue to put band-aids over gaping wounds, fooling themselves into believing that business could continue as usual.

Catherine got this message, too. Unlike me, though, she chose to join the corporate office on the path of least resistance. Faced with a decision between standing up for what was right and keeping her job, she saved herself. She had been physically present for every incident, and she knew all of the stories of Nick's inappropriate behavior. She had even provided me with much of the documentation. And yet, when corporate asked her to support Nick rather than advocating for his removal from the company, her response was to acquiesce. She remained reluctant to take any action that would challenge the status quo.

I did not. A few months later, I resigned from a job I had once loved, where I had spent years building and growing. Robert Frost minimizes reluctance as a rational response to change and loss. But for me, peace and safety were more important than a job. This experience required I finally come to grips with the fact that change was necessary. While it took some time to process this, I finally truly resigned. I chose to "yield with a grace," as Frost puts it.

RELUCTANCE

In many ways, it's easier to process the meanings of Nick's toxicity than to come to terms with the complicity of Catherine, Human Resources, and the corporation in general. As I have pointed out in previous chapters, the costs of toxic leadership are difficult to dismiss both in terms of economics and the emotional stability of the workplace community. So how could Catherine stand by silently as Nick's toxic behavior - behavior that could easily have been a legal liability - was tolerated? How could she fail to stand with me and demand that he be removed from his position? The answer lies in the human response of reluctance.

It is natural to value stability in our lives. We want to feel in control of our work lives, and as a result, many of us shy away from conflicts. We avoid jeopardizing our ability to stay in our jobs, even when we realize this decision is harmful to ourselves and others. This is reluctance. In situations of toxic leadership, reluctance shows up in our tendency to fantasize about a time when things will be better. Sometimes it shows up in our rationalization of the leaders' behavior, or as subtle mental attitudes that blame victims or incorrectly assign equal responsibility to "both sides." At its core, reluctance is the avoidance of doing the right thing, whether that be reporting, advocating for the removal of a leader, or resigning, and we tend to turn to reluctance when we fear the consequences of standing up to toxic leadership more than we fear that toxicity itself.

However, while this reluctance is both common and understandable, it is not just. By its very nature, it represents complicity in the harms of toxic leaders to ourselves, our co-workers, and, in the case of Human Resources managers, the workers we are meant to protect. In this chapter, I highlight the meanings of reluctance in hopes that it will help Human Resources managers, employees, and leaders to recognize reluctance in themselves and others. It is a dangerous thing to sit in the space of reluctance for too long.

We cannot fully appreciate how common, or how damaging, reluctance can be without first exploring the complicity at its heart. Toxic leaders cannot maintain power without followers, and these followers are often characterized by a deep sense of reluctance to change. We will proceed, then, by exploring the impact of followers in a toxic workplace setting.

The Toxic Follower

As I have discussed in detail earlier, employees who find themselves subordinated to a toxic leader experience a host of negative life impacts. One study, led by Professor John Schaubroek of the Robert J. Trulaske, Sr. College of Business at the University of Missouri, described toxic leaders as excessively demanding and personally insensitive. In this study, toxic leaders demonstrated traits of hostility, characterized by blaming others, sowing mistrust, and using destructive feedback to tear down their employees.[34] This behavior, Schaubroek and his colleagues argue, was linked to characteristics of neuroticism, with toxic leaders often displaying behaviors that indicated moodiness, anxiety, frustrations and fear. As in my own experience, these leaders' followers reported a multitude of personal harms as a result of exposure to toxicity, ranging from emotional distress to psychological upset, and even physical symptoms like gastric problems, hair loss, headaches, and other illnesses.[35]

Giving these damaging experiences, it may seem harsh to focus on how workers, who are generally victims of toxic leadership, contribute to the harmful behaviors of toxic leaders. And yet, research show us that leaders' power can only exist when followers are willing to support and enable their behaviors. In healthy workplaces, we might describe this behavior as employee engagement, morale, or loyalty. Unfortunately, these are the very behaviors that toxic leaders use to manipulate employees and bypass the formal disciplinary mechanisms of Human Resources. For example, in Schaubroek's study, toxic leaders often used destructive feedback mechanisms, ranging from yelling to passive-aggressive comments about workplace performance, as a way of using an employee's loyalty and engagement against them.[36] Since these employees wanted to do well, they were willing to put up with the verbal abuse, sometimes believing that it was deserved. When examined in this way, it becomes clear that employee dedication and loyalty, typically considered positive traits, are easily used by toxic leaders to manipulate workers into becoming *toxic followers*. A toxic follower is an employee who is reluctant to stand up to a toxic leader, instead engaging in enabling behaviors ranging from avoiding the leader altogether to participating in the leader's counterproductive work behaviors.

When placed in a situation of toxic leadership that an employee is unwilling to leave, workers must find ways to cope. In a 2016 study, workplace psychology expert Dr. Vicki Webster and her team broadly surveyed victims of toxic leadership. Workers indicated a variety of coping strategies, ranging from strategic venting to total avoidance.[37] One common tactic involved venting about toxic behaviors with trusted colleagues, an approach that allowed employees to process their experiences without actually confronting the toxic leader or the leader's superiors. Other victims chose to take a leave of absence from the company, perhaps hoping that time might fix the leaders' behavior, or perhaps just needing to heal from the psychological and physical damage they had experienced. An understandable but disappointing commonality among these coping strategies is the failure to hold toxic leaders accountable. Since most coping behaviors happen out of earshot of the toxic leader, their behavior is able to continue unabated.

When it comes to workplace toxicity, there is a very fine line between victim and follower. As a study from the Department of management, Innovation, and Entrepreneurship at North Carolina State University explains, workers who take on the role of complicity to the toxic leader often become even more susceptible to that leaders' toxicity. The continued toxicity then prompts more complicity, and can even escalate to collusion and participation in the counterproductive work behaviors. Within this cycle of abuse and complicity, victims grow to feel increasingly powerless. Fearing social exclusion, many choose to quit their jobs.[38] Others lean in to the role of toxic follower, actively or passively participating in the harmful behaviors of the leader. Often, followers of toxic leaders choose to report behaviors only anecdotally, to coworkers and colleagues rather than through the company's formal channels, or not at all.[39]

Given the extreme negative consequences of toxic leadership on employees, how can we explain the failure of Human Resources to step in and help? Previous research has asserted that, while Human Resources professionals take bullying seriously, the issue of toxic leadership appeared complex and insurmountable to them.[40] Even though it is common for organizations to have the types of policies that could be used to stop toxic leadership, these policies are often vague, in that they are overly open to interpretation and make no mention of bullying or other explicit forms of aggression.[41] Fearing that this imprecise wording could lead to legal challenges, local Human Resources professionals often (correctly) believe that any disciplinary action they take based on these policies could be rejected by corporate HR, reversing the disciplinary action and leaving them even more vulnerable to the toxic leader in their workplace. These policies represent the primary source of institutional power for lower-level Human Resources representatives. As a result, many Human Resources professionals feel powerless to deal with these behaviors.

However, whether or not Human Resources professionals *feel* powerless in situations of toxic leadership, they are in fact better poised to handle the situation than many other employees. By definition, HR professionals monitor job satisfaction, turnover, employee motivation, and employee perception. They are tasked with proactively monitoring the firm's culture with the goal of increasing the organization's performance. From the leadership perspective, since HR professionals are involved in hiring, terminations, training, and development, individuals in this role are best positioned to spot toxicity and counterproductive work behaviors as they develop. From the employee perspective, and perhaps more importantly, Human Resources is the primary mechanism of resolving employee-related plights.[42] A position in Human Resources, then, is perhaps one of responsibility rather than power. HR managers, particularly at the local level, may not have the power to protect their workers, but they have the responsibility to try.

One important, but often overlooked, way that Human Resources could better equip themselves for the challenges of toxic leadership is through consistent and credible continuing education. In a University of Iowa study funded by the Society for Human Resources Management, professor Sara L. Rynes and colleagues found that a high percentage of HR professionals had failed to receive sufficient training on the field's best practices, including new techniques for preventing toxic leaders from rising to power in an organization.[43] In fact, these researchers found, that HR professionals tended to answer confidently about various research-based aspects of their jobs, such as the use of personality assessments in hiring and promotion decisions, even when a sizable portion of their responses was demonstrably incorrect. Perhaps even more concerning, this study demonstrated that the areas of confusion were *not* trivial issues. Instead, the researchers note,

> the biggest gaps between research findings and practitioner beliefs concern some of the most central issues in HR: first, how to choose the best employees and, second, how to effectively motivate them through appropriate goal-setting and effective performance management.[44]

In other words, the largest gaps in knowledge for Human Resources professionals were areas that align with toxic leadership, first through careful hiring and promotional practices and second through the actual tools of leadership. As Professor Rynes noted, Human Resources professionals who do not understand the necessary tools for addressing issues like toxic leadership are highly unlikely to utilize those tools effectively.[45]

Human resources practices and management must not only ensure that the human capital is sufficient, in terms of skills and relational competencies for the organization, but that it also remains sufficient.[46] Human capital and the resulting labor costs are the largest of organizational operating expenses. A company's human resources or human capital is also imperative to competitive advantage. Yet little research exists that gives a voice to human resources management's efforts on measuring, managing, and mitigating toxic leadership, leaving Human Resources professionals with the monumental task of maintaining a healthy and safe work environment while often failing to provide these important employees with the continuing education and training to effectively do so.

Most corporate offices assume that lower-level HR professionals are equipped and ready to handle any and all intra-office personnel problems that emerge. HR performance management efforts could provide an early indication of workplace toxicity. Their ability to accomplish these goals is, however, limited to individual and organizational competency and the ways in which the individual and organization view the role of Human Resources. When Human Resources professionals are reluctant to stop a toxic leader, they become the most dangerous kind of toxic follower. And yet, in my experience interviewing Human Resources professionals, I found them to be kind, well-meaning individuals who recognized the harmful nature of toxic leadership and who wanted to help. We can best understand the complex nature of *unintentional toxic followers* by considering the role of reluctance in the day-to-day experiences of toxic leadership as they affect general employees as well as Human Resources professionals.

What is Reluctance?

Researcher Leah Hollis describes workplace toxicity as similar to the act of a "petty thief ... stealing productivity and causing employee disengagement."[47] This type of disengagement can create the appearance that an organization is maintaining human capital, in that the number of employees remains stable, while in actuality the potential success of a workplace is in a downward spiral. In other words, tenure at an organization is not equivalent to engagement. In fact, a 2019 Forbes Magazine study revealed that over one-third of employees surveyed planned to resign and look for a new job.[48] However, of that group, only 21% reported feeling highly engaged at work. This means that over one-quarter of employees surveyed in the Forbes study were doing just enough to avoid being fired. If we generalize this finding to the workplace population, one out of every four employees are doing little more than collecting a paycheck. But why are so many people stuck in jobs that are, at best, disengaging, and at worst, toxic? The answer lies in reluctance.

Reluctance can take on many forms in the toxic workplace, but its effect is always the same. As employees grow more and more aware of the problems of toxic leadership, they simultaneously become less engaged, leading to higher absenteeism, lower productivity, and, as a result, lower profitability. Translated into monetary value, disengagement costs companies approximately 34% of the employee's annual salary, but it costs employees even more. The experiences described by my research participants, as well as my own experiences, are all examples of social injustices that take place in the cast of a toxic leadership system. These social injustices have the potential to rip away dreams and cause oppression to individuals and their families.

The warning signs of reluctance that are common to both general employees and Human Resources professionals include *low morale, feelings of helplessness, withdrawal, increased gossip and venting,* and *mentally quitting.* In addition, those working in HR under a toxic leader may experience what I call *collateral damage.*

Low Morale

As I stated in previous chapters, leaders have a significant impact on morale. Leader behavior, positive and negative, is among the most influential. Supportive behaviors provide motivation that result in productive and engaged employees. Toxic behaviors do just the opposite. On an individual level, morale encompasses things like an employee's engagement, mood, job performance, and psychological well-being. When an employee becomes a victim of the leader's toxic behaviors, the performance, health, and financial wellbeing of the employee, organization, and other stakeholders suffer.

This was certainly the case for Angela, a Human Resources manager who watched the general mood of her organization deteriorate before her eyes. The toxic leader at the head of her company, she told me, "destroyed morale." Once this leader took the helm, and his toxic traits began to seep through the workplace, Angela observed that her organization became a revolving door of new employees. Try as she might, she was unable to hire and retain new employees, as the general mood among longer tenured workers was so low.

Feelings of Helplessness

While all of the professionals I spoke with understood the damage a toxic leader imposed, most participants felt they lacked the power to stop the abusive and counterproductive work behaviors they saw spreading throughout their organization. When asked to describe consequences toxic leaders face due to their behavior, an alarming number of participants agreed, "not enough ever happens outside of training." Just as my boss, Nick, had been enrolled multiple times in anger management training, but continued to wreak havoc on our office, many of the professionals in my study reported that the corporate directive was toward trainings. This allowed people at the top of the organization to feign responsibility and care while avoiding any hard decisions that might actually discipline the toxic leaders appropriately. This type of "tightrope act," in which Human Resource managers are responsible for "managing" toxic leaders without being granted the power or authority to do so, can result in a sense of helplessness in HR professionals and others.

This was certainly the case of Jada, a Human Resources professional I interviewed. Jada told me that she had "written handbooks and numerous policies" in attempt to mitigate and prevent toxic leadership from spreading. And yet, she observed case after case in which a toxic leader violated the HR policy only to be given a pass. As she explained, "there should not be any room in business for a toxic leader. This is an oxymoron. You cannot be toxic and a leader." But as it became clear that upper management was unwilling to enforce these policies without bias, her feelings of helplessness grew.

Withdrawal

Organizations require a productive and engaged staff to accomplish goals. Engaged employees are more likely to spawn creativity and innovation. They understand business needs and work with coworkers to improve the organization and accomplish goals. On the contrast, disengaged employees often become withdrawn, choosing to isolate themselves rather than risk angering the toxic leader.

Breanna's experience working in a technical education organization illustrated the potential for toxic leadership to cause workers to withdraw. She shared that she and her coworkers "constantly dealt with verbal abuse from management and unproductive leaders above those managers" in which the toxic leaders "took pleasure in

humiliating their employees in front of other employees."
As damaging as this behavior was for all employees, what
happened next only added to the struggle. In Breanna's
workplace, this direct verbal abuse resulted in "factions and
an everybody for themselves sort of attitude." Employees
withdrew either into themselves or into group that they
believed would provide some protection from the toxic
leader, resulting in a workplace that lacked collaboration or
community.

Increased Gossip and Venting

Just as the toxic leader in Breanna's workplace
caused employees to break off into factions, the occurrence
of increased gossip and venting is common in workplaces
headed by a toxic leader. In fact, most participants in my
research lack formal tools for identifying toxic leaders.
Instead, their discoveries of toxic leadership often relied on
employee complaints, venting, and workplace gossip.
While activities like venting are important aspects of any

organization, including healthy workplaces, Callie pointed out that too much venting and gossip can "drain energy from the real work of the organization."

The toxic behaviors of Callie's dysfunctional boss often included things like mood swings, slamming of doors, racial slurs, and harsh criticism. The unpredictability of her toxic leader's moods meant that employees weren't certain what to expect from him each day. As a survival strategy, she told me, employees often whispered amongst themselves, checking in with each other to ask, "Have you spoken to him?" or "Is he in a good mood?" When these attempts to avoid their toxic leader were unsuccessful, Callie and her coworkers, after toxic encounters, often "scurried off and found someone to lick their wounds." As a result, much time was wasted on recovering from this toxic leader's counterproductive work behaviors, rather than focusing on achieving goals.

Mentally Quitting

Organizations should not assume tenure equates to job satisfaction. Equally, organizations must be cognizant of the fact that disengagement or quitting mentally is equally, if not more, damaging than quitting physically. When employees quit mentally, they do so in their mind. Since this type of resignation is not verbal or physical, it can be difficult to tell when an employee has ceased contributing to the company's success, and to the workplace in general.

In my own experience, workplace toxicity exposed me to new and sometimes unfamiliar elements of my character, many of which I am not proud of. On any given day, I was a strong woman behaving weakly, a smart woman searching for basic words, a hardworking woman spitefully slacking on the job, an intuitive woman unable to formulate thoughts to make simple decisions. With great reluctance, I quit work, but, I didn't exactly resign from my position.

RELUCTANCE

This type of resignation is common among employees of toxic leaders. Employees are motivated by a large variety of factors, and the more vulnerable an employee is in society, the more important external rewards, like a paycheck or job security, become. For example, people from working class or poor backgrounds may not have the option to actually quit a job, since they lack the safety net of accumulated wealth. Racial discrimination may also prevent people from formally resigning from a job, given that the risk of not being hired at a similar level of professionalism is more common among racially marginalized workers. Therefore, it is common for economic motivations to overshadow our basic human need for safety and emotional security, leading employees to feel reluctant about the possibility of actually quitting.

Collateral Damage

In speaking with Human Resources managers about the ways toxic leadership impacted their workplaces, one accidental finding emerged. While I had expected to collect information about the employees they supported, I found that many Human Resources professionals also experienced severe ramifications from toxic leaders. In fact, often when Human Resources managers tried to intervene into toxic workplaces, they often experienced collateral damage, either by becoming the target of the toxic leader themselves or through the indirect consequences of the toxicity. In the end, the vast majority of the Human Resources professionals I interviewed reported being a personal target of a toxic leader.

Makayla, a Human Resources manager I interviewed, put this best when she noted,

> An important part of the equation is that HR professionals have bosses too. Therefore, even when Human Resources managers know the laws,

rules, and regulations, and even when they report toxic leaders to their bosses, often their hands are tied by those at the top of the corporate food chain. At this point, a Human Resources professional has only two choices. They can stand up to their boss(es), appealing to their own moral compass and values, and following the law to the best of their ability. Or they can attempt to find a workaround, seeking out creative ways to smoothing things over with an employee or break through to the toxic leader. These choices force a decision between protecting the interests of the company or protecting the employees in your workplace.

Being put in this position can create stress and strain on Human Resources managers and, as collateral damage, on their families and home lives. This decision often presents itself as a no-win situation. As Makayla told me, "sometimes the answer or solution is not very clear cut on what can be done to manage both." Makayla saw her role in HR as "a 'sounding board' ... there to protect the company and the employee." And yet, even when she attempted to intervene, begging the toxic leader to change, her experience told her that "these types of managers do not often heed your advice ahead of time. They only come back for help once the situation spirals out of control." Often, she told me, employees would quit, sometimes bringing a lawsuit against the company, and the company would settle to "avoid a spread of news about the [manager's] behavior."

Like Makayla, many HR managers reported that they are given a responsibility to mitigate leader toxicity but are often not given the authority to do so. As a result, when Human Resources filed a report against a leader, that report was unlikely to result in serious discipline, but often meant that the HR professional became a target for the toxic leader themselves. As Makayla recounted with some sadness, "After I realized what was happening, I suggested as much. [My manager] took personal offense and stated I was attacking her credibility. I was fired shortly following...."

As reluctance emerges in each of these unique ways, it becomes clear that it is much too simplistic to simply place the blame for toxic leadership on Human Resources professionals. Instead, we must understand that reluctance is something that can impact us all. Whether we feel powerless to solve the problem or believe that we are helping by venting to our coworkers, all of these behaviors come down to a reluctance to do what is needed to remove ourselves from the toxic workplace and, perhaps, inspire others to do the same.

The Costs of Reluctance and Benefits of Giving Up

Reluctance, as described in Robert Frost's poem, is about a natural stubbornness. It is about the sense that accepting change, "the end of a … season" in Frost's words, is akin to giving up. Of course, Frost's poem has deep roots in the ways we, as a society, think about work. "Keep trying. Don't give up," we tell children. "Nothing worth having comes easy." This type of message sinks deep inside of our psyche, and as adults, we tell ourselves and our coworkers to "hang in there." Frost's poem describes our battle with the shifting seasons of life as human nature, framing the idea of fighting against change as an inherent virtue. And while Frost argues that reluctance is rational, a natural part of grieving, in many cases reluctance is extremely irrational behavior. In the case of a toxic workplace, there is a high cost to reluctance and often a great benefit to giving up.

As I have discussed in this chapter, Reluctance takes on many forms, often encouraging employees to disconnect, isolate, or participate in the hostile environment sparked by their toxic leaders. While these reactions are understandable, they are harmful in their complicity. In cases like these, often the only option is to give up. Despite the cultural stigma against giving up, by removing yourself from the toxic environment, you give yourself permission to be a whole person, living not only for your work, but also for your personal, emotional, and spiritual health. By giving up reluctance, you give yourself permission to move on to the next step: *healing.*

Chapter Four

Healing

If you want to fly, you got to give up the shit that weighs you down.

Toni Morrison

The company I worked for was not always a breeding ground for toxic leadership. For over a decade, I'm told, the company's founders worked hard to inspire a culture of family, respect, and social support. These values influenced not only the daily experiences of employees, but also decisions about compensation and promotion. In other words, the organizational culture was reinforced by the architecture of the company. The company put its money where its mouth was, so to speak.

Approximately one year after I began working for the company, it was sold. As gradual changes unfolded over the years following, it became clear to me that I had become trapped in a toxic environment that bore little resemblance to the organization I had been hired into.

A year or so after I found the courage to resign, a former colleague invited me to join her for lunch. She and I had worked together in the company years before, and she was shocked to learn about Nick's behaviors. Although I was proud to tell her that I had finally stood up for myself, I noted that my heart still felt heavy.

"Thank God time heals all wounds," she said. "I'm so glad you're doing okay now."

I nodded and smiled, blinking back tears. The simple act of recounting my experiences with toxic leadership had left my heart palpitating and my fingers fidgeting. I prayed she couldn't see the pain and trauma I'd been carrying for the past year.

I left that lunch feeling a bit perplexed. After all, I had conquered toxic leadership. I had emerged from the company the victor, refusing to allow Nick to abuse me while Catherine stood by. I was proud of the courage I'd found to resign. And yet, I questioned whether my former colleague was correct. Does time truly heal everything?

There may be *some* truth to the phrase. However, when it comes to healing from toxic leadership, one size certainly does not fit all. Perhaps, for some, time can heal wounds through the opportunities it affords to build new skills and reframe our experiences. Time allows us to build perspective on difficult events, because we inevitably experience new struggles and triumphs. I had certainly tried this while I was still employed with the company. Once I realized that Nick's pattern of abuse was not simply a matter of him "having a moment," I sought out trainings to deal with the situation. I tried to aid the role of time by learning new techniques to put the situation into perspective. One training advocated the idea that "life is 10% what happens to you and 90% how you react to it." But when I went back to work, armed with this new perspective, I felt disappointed. Even when I tried to adjust my own behavior to compensate for the abuse I was experiencing, Nick's toxicity persisted. Time could not help as long as I remained.

Or, perhaps time can heal us through the fading of our memories. As we move on in our lives, the hurt begins to feel much less immediate. I had experienced this with other difficult periods in my life, but somehow this trauma felt different. When I had lunch with my former colleague, a year after I'd resigned from the company, I was still experiencing overwhelming symptoms as a result of my traumatic encounter with a toxic leader. I endured flashbacks of events, insomnia, panic attacks, and even a mental resistance to working in a traditional workspace. In fact, I still periodically experience these negative impacts of Nick's toxicity. While I am not qualified to diagnose post-traumatic stress disorder, or PTSD, I cannot ignore how closely these symptoms resemble the disorder. And whether or not my experiences fall under the umbrella of PTSD, these recurring maladies certainly illustrate that time could not heal my particular workplace wounds.

As I turned over my former colleague's words in my mind, I realized that my experiences went beyond everyday struggle. I hadn't simply had a difficult period at work. My experiences with toxic leadership had encoded themselves onto my heart and mind. They were imprinted on me as lingering trauma. And while I don't begrudge those who are able to heal from workplace toxicity simply through the passing of time, it became clear to me that I needed to work much more actively toward healing. It was through this realization that I came to understand what was required for me to move forward in my journey to healing.

For me, healing required that I first get a good understanding of my experience. In my journey to healing, I revisited the origin of Nick's toxicity. This time I wanted to move beyond justifying his behavior to instead lean in to an explanation of my own experience as a trauma. Justification is shallow, offering an excuse and even permission for behavior. Understanding, which is required for healing, goes deep to explain root causes of an action. To move beyond justification to understanding, I found that I needed to accept a *sufficient* understanding, realizing that

I would never receive an explanation or apology from Nick. Instead, I needed to focus on myself, opening my heart to new opportunities. I realized that holding on to the secrets of this experience was weighing me down, so I took a cue from Toni Morrison. I finally decided to "give up the shit that [was weighing me] down."

After I'd reflected on the adage that "time heals all wounds," particularly in terms of my experience with toxic leadership, I realized that this expression is much too passive to truly capture what is necessary for victims of workplace toxicity to heal. Recall that toxic leadership results in a range of physical and mental "wounds," ranging from hair loss and IBS to panic attacks. These are actual illnesses, and as such, it is unrealistic for most of us to imagine that time alone will heal them. Instead, the residue of toxic leadership requires victims to take a proactive role in the process of healing. It requires us to understand that the things that happened to us, and the remaining traces of that trauma, are real. It requires us to excavate our memories and reexamine the things we justified, dismissed, or buried in the recesses of our minds, and seek out healing strategies that best match our needs.

Trauma is unique. Likewise, the healing process is different for everyone. I suggest that time does *not* heal all wounds. Rather, time used *efficiently* heals all wounds. In this chapter, I urge those who are still struggling to unpack the residual trauma of toxicity and to finally take the steps required to heal. We must find ways of moving forward with understanding, not as a way of justifying the harms of toxic leadership, but as a way of releasing the anger and other negative feelings that control us - the "shit that weighs you down." This process of understanding is all-inclusive, and it should encompass multiple components of the situation, recognizing that toxic leadership is a complex process that requires complicity on the part of many players and organizations. By understanding what happened to us, we can work to let go of the toxic residue that still sticks with us. Only then can we open our hearts to new opportunities with our minds prepared to embrace them.

To truly heal from the experiences of toxic leadership, we must first acknowledge that to live through a toxic workplace is to experience trauma. Often I find that people who have lived through the nightmare of toxic leadership, including myself, are hesitant to describe what they've been through as trauma, worrying that the word is too extreme or should be reserved for those who have had a formal psychiatric diagnosis. But embracing an understanding of our experience as trauma allows us to better unpack the feelings we have as we heal.

Why All the Fuss, It's Just a Job Right?

Perhaps when you think of trauma, you imagine the post-traumatic responses of soldiers who have returned from war. In fact, although psychologists now understand that trauma can stem from a variety of negative experiences, the concept emerged from World War II veterans who returned with what was then called "shell shock."[49] This early understanding of trauma was somewhat simplistic, leading scholars to refer to it as a "lay theory." As trauma scholar Jeffrey C. Alexander writes, lay theory understands traumas as "naturally occurring events that shatter an individual or collective actor's sense of well-being."[50] This understanding of trauma was deeply invested in understanding trauma as an extension of human nature, which led psychologists of the time to understand trauma as a breakdown of the mind. The goal of therapy at this time, then, was to rebuild or restore the patient's understanding of the world as a safe place, despite the victim's knowledge and experiences that illustrated otherwise.[51]

The idea that trauma responses are guided by the individual's interpretation of the situation eventually lead to an understanding of trauma called "enlightenment

."[52] In this approach, psychologists reframed the relationship between the mind and the trauma, shifting from the previous understanding of the trauma as a shattering event to a new way of seeing trauma responses as reasonable responses to a legitimately perceived threat. In other words, this approach validated victim's understandings of the trauma. Rather than focusing on whether or not a patient understands an event as traumatic, then, the enlightenment approach suggests that healing requires a different interpretation. In other words, the way individuals interpret or process a situation eventually leads to the extent to which they perceive the situation as stressful.[53] Psychologist Richard Lazarus further explains this concept, in his 1966 book, *Psychological Stress and Coping Process*, arguing that stress differs significantly based on how we interpret events and our appraisal of those events.[54] Individuals who suffer with PTSD process trauma in a way that leads to a sense of serious and current threat.

Eventually, enlightenment thinking would lead psychologists into the approach to trauma that comes to mind when most people imagine therapy: psychoanalytic thinking. Under this approach, championed by psychologist Saul Friendländer in 1979, trauma should be treated not only by resolving issues of the outside world, but also by focusing on the healing of the internal sense of self.[55] It is from this perspective that we get the commonly circulated idea that we cannot change the way others behave; we can only change the way we respond. Understanding trauma as something that lives within the bodies of victims resulted in three important directions for future work in the area of individual and cultural trauma.[56] These three points continue to function as the foundation for the understanding and treatment of trauma, and they are useful for making sense of how toxic leadership contributes to mental, emotional, and physical maladies even after the victim has been removed from the traumatic situation.

First, the psychoanalytic approach to trauma helped to solidify an idea first introduced by enlightenment thinkers: the idea that a patient can make great strides toward healing when they are prompted to unpack and reframe the event. The importance of this premise for toxic leadership cannot be overstated. Working with professor of practice, John Murtagh, deputy director of the National Cancer Control Initiative, Brian R. McAvoy referred to workplace bullying as "the silent epidemic."[57] For McAvoy and Murtagh, toxic leadership often grows out of control quickly because those affected tend to remain silent. In their research, they find that workers employed by toxic leaders tend to exhibit "dysfunction, fear, shame, and embarrassment," indicating that these victims are experiencing the trauma of workplace toxicity not as an external stressor, but as an internal failure.[58] It should come as no surprise, then, that those who experience this internalized blame for workplace toxicity are unlikely to escape from their environment and even less likely to heal.

Recall that the key to healing trauma for enlightenment and psychoanalytic thinkers is the unpacking and reframing of the experiences of trauma. This approach was the impetus for a 2008 University of Washington study that tested the treatment of stress-related symptoms with a therapy called "*Cognitive Reappraisal.*"[59] *Cognitive reappraisal* is a form of psychological treatment that involves victims of trauma attempting to make sense of their experiences. This can include a recounting or reassessment of the events, followed by a short pause to reflect. *Cognitive reappraisal*, the authors note, is particularly useful in circumstances that involve *expressive suppression*, or what is colloquially referred to as bottling up your emotions. Staying silent about one's trauma only creates more negative effects, including depression and anxiety. Talking through the experiences of trauma, on the

147

other hand, allow patients to heal and move forward in the healthiest manner possible.

Second, the psychoanalytic approach to trauma eventually led to an understanding of trauma as something that imprints itself on the body, including the brain. It is from this perspective that our contemporary understanding of post-traumatic stress disorder, or PTSD, emerges. Understanding trauma as something that can actually change the way the brain functions is useful in considering treatments of trauma that target underlying issues. Dr. Ruth Lanius, of the University of Western Ontario in Canada, has performed extensive research on this area. Lanius argues that traumatic memories are actually imprinted and stored in the brain in very specific ways.[60] This means that recalling these memories functions in a physiologically different way than recalling ordinary, non-traumatic experiences. Whereas other memories may fade over time, or even gain a sense of joyful nostalgia, traumatic memories tend to remain psychologically upsetting long after the event passes. In some cases, in fact, PTSD can last a lifetime.

Finally, and perhaps most central to my approach in this book, the psychoanalytic perspective on trauma tells us that understanding patterns of trauma response behavior can be helpful not only for psychologists, but also for patients. It is certainly important for psychotherapists to understand the common ways people process trauma, the contemporary approach to the psychoanalytic treatment of trauma recognizes that it is important for victims to understand that they are not alone. When we understand that our patterns of processing trauma are similar to others' experiences, we are better able to identify our own trauma responses and adjust our framing of events accordingly. By understanding how others respond to traumatic scenarios similar to our own, we can proactively approach these situations *as* trauma. We can learn from others, as well as formal research, and help to build up our own defenses against post-traumatic responses. And, importantly, we can process our experiences with a degree of distance, and recognize when it is time to seek help.

Take It Back

The title of this book centers my survival after my experiences with toxic leadership. But surviving does not mean emerging unscathed. As I have recounted throughout this book, my extended encounters with toxic leadership left me with numerous psychological scars that come alarmingly close to descriptions of PTSD. And I am not alone. In his discussion of the results of the 2014 Workplace Bullying Survey, Gary Namie of the Workplace Bullying Institute suggests that PTSD is often an overlooked diagnosis for victims of counterproductive workplace behaviors.[61]

My own research supports Namie's assertion and adds chilling anecdotes to underscore the residue of trauma that lingers after the experience of working under a toxic leader. Several study participants saw moving on and or healing as the opportunity to "take back" power. This idea of actively taking back something that was stolen offers a sense of hopefulness and demonstrates the underlying belief that healing is possible, even when it is not easy. It also indicates the acknowledgement of toxic leadership experiences as a trauma. In fact, Shelby likened her experience to the trauma of sexual assault. After her daunting experience working as a Human Resources manager under a toxic leader, she decided to leave the field altogether. She told me " I felt like a rape victim, picking up my clothes, running away from the scene naked, beaten, afraid, yet grateful to be free." Of course, I do not mean to draw equivalencies between the experience of rape and the experience of toxic leader abuse. Doing so is unnecessary and unproductive. Both are horrific experiences, and both leave their own traces of trauma.

Rather, I include Shelby's quote because it is exemplary of some of the participants I interviewed, individuals who understood that toxic leadership is an experience of power imbalance. Similar to perpetrators of sexual abuse, Shelby told me, the toxic leader she'd worked under was motivated by a need for dominance and control. As we discussed her situation, she shared many ideas that were similar to others in my study. In particular, as I discussed in Chapter 3, she acknowledged having surrendered her power to the leader, however unconsciously. She had served him as an unwitting follower, propping up his behavior for the years she worked under him. Her experience was not unlike my own. Both of us surrendered, though not willingly or consciously. In moving past the experience, though, we both saw the imperative to take back power in a conscious, purposeful, and swift move toward healing.

Participants like Shelby immediately acknowledged the pain and suffering caused by a toxic leader and described seeking therapy to heal from their experiences. Other participants, however, described their experiences with toxic leadership, but seemed reluctant to acknowledge the pain and suffering it caused them. As we spoke, the layers of shame and toughness peeled back, eventually revealing a full account of the trauma they had experienced and the residue that trauma left behind. I recognized these barriers because I'd frequently used them myself.

While toxic leaders do not limit their victims by race, gender, sexual orientation, or other demographic categories, these outward identities do influence the particular experiences we have with toxicity. And in fact, the barriers of shame, toughness, and resistance to seeking help - barriers I recognized in myself - emerged most often in my African American participants. Research is clear and abundant on the adverse mental health outcomes of all people who are subjected to toxicity. But there are well noted and alarming racial and gender differences in the perception and processing of workplace bullying and toxicity. People of color may be less likely to seek help, internalizing the stereotypes of unflinching strength that are often heaped onto Black women, and unfortunately we are more likely to find ourselves targets of abuse[62] and less likely to feel supported by the buffering mechanism of coworker social support.[63] These issues make it even more important that people of color and women seek out support in the process of healing.

Given the differences in experiences of toxic leadership, and quite simply the unique ways trauma is experienced by each individual person, it can be difficult to offer blanket recommendations of ways to approach the healing process. For me, though, recognizing that I was undergoing a process of grief was key in my path toward healing. This process emerged over and over in my research participants as well.

In her 1969 book *On Death and Dying,* Elisabeth Kübler-Ross revealed five stages of grief: denial and isolation, anger, bargaining, depression, and acceptance. Based on her experiences working with people with terminal illnesses, the book describes stages of grief that may not be experienced in the same way or the same order by all people. Remember, trauma is unique. Still, psychologists agree that these stages often appear in those coping with trauma, and they can be helpful for making sense of the feelings that emerge in those healing after experiences with toxic leadership.

Denial and Isolation

Research confirms the notion of grieving, like what's experienced during death, is common among participants/survivors of workplace toxicity.[64] In the denial and isolation stage, victims fight the reality of the experience. Denial and isolation can take the form of reluctance, the topic of the previous chapter.

When denial is experienced as reluctance, it can prevent victims from leaving a bad situation. The abusive situation of toxic leadership is a trauma, and as such, it can understandably leave victims cloaked in doubt and self-blame. This was the case in my own experience, as I often attempted to justify Nick's behavior, even considering whether I was to blame for the situation. As skilled manipulators, toxic leaders often harness the denial stage as a way to maintain their power, as when Nick told me, "I always viewed you as stronger than this." Realizing that my personality made it likely that I would internalize his counterproductive work behaviors as partially my own fault, he harnessed my denial.

As a result, I hesitated to share my experiences with others. After all, I reasoned, if my behavior was contributing to the toxicity in my workplace, it would only make me look bad to tell others about the situation. I even hesitated to share the full experience with my former colleague during our lunch date. Choosing not to correct her when she assumed that I had healed from the abuse, I allowed her to believe that the toxic situation was far less traumatic than it actually was. This type of denial only exacerbates feelings of isolation, a common sentiment among the survivors of toxic leadership that I interviewed in my research.

Denial can also take on other forms more generally related to the experience of trauma. Often denial takes on the shape of *expressive suppression*. Victims bottle up their emotions in the conscious or unconscious hope that ignoring the negative feelings might make them go away. Unfortunately, the habitual use of expressive suppression has been linked to experiences of depression, anxiety, and even PTSD.[65] *Expressive suppression* is generally treated through a guided practice of *cognitive reappraisal,* in which victims attempt to reinterpret or process a situation. Through *cognitive reappraisal*, victims might attempt to make sense of what's happening to them. This can include a recount or reassessment of the events and a short pause to reflect. Importantly, though, reappraisal is a very different process from rumination, and it is important that cognitive reappraisal does not end in justification or prolonged reluctance.

Anger

For victims of toxic leadership, the anger stage can be very helpful. Particular for those who have suppressed their feelings of trauma, finally working through the anger and injustice of the toxic experience is an important step toward healing. This stage is characterized by victims losing their ability to mask their feelings. They look for blame and deflect anger accordingly. Victims experiencing the anger stage may act out of their natural character.

When I was experiencing the anger stage, I found myself purposefully slacking, claiming agency by working ineffectively as a way of passively lashing out against Nick. I am typically a very diligent worker, even tending toward perfectionism, so this was unusual for me. I felt angry at Nick for his treatment, but I knew I could not directly lash out at him. Therefore, my anger stage had to take on much more indirect forms.

Reflecting on some of the conversations I had with Nick over the years prior to his turn toward toxic leadership, I truly wonder whether his abuse was a result of his unprocessed anger about his own experiences of working under a toxic leader. He would often recount stories of verbal and emotional abuse from an earlier time when he worked for his father. Hurt people hurt people, and perhaps Nick's toxic behavior was a result of his own failure to heal himself.

Dr. Margaret E. Gary

That said, this stage of processing trauma should not be confused with the angry forms of denial we often see from toxic leaders and their toxic followers. While toxic leaders may themselves be victims of trauma, my reference here to anger is limited to the processing of trauma. I, however, certainly hope that Nick and Catherine are someday able to process their own issues, their retaliation against me and others who came forward with stories of Nick's toxicity and Catherine's complicity.

Fortunately, labor laws are in place to protect witnesses from retaliation, especially in the form of termination. However, protection is limited in these laws, as they fail to account for the depth and power of manipulation. When corporate Human Resources pressured Catherine to support Nick, rather than come forward with her account of the abuse she had witnessed, she deflected her anger toward me. She was angry that I had spoken up,

160

perhaps using anger to cover feelings of guilt for her role as a toxic follower.

Catherine was not the only witness who played part in attempting to mitigate Nick's toxicity. I suspect there was unjust sharing, with Nick, of names of those who acted as witnesses to my complaints. These supportive coworkers, and fellow victims of Nick's toxicity, also experienced a masked form of retaliation. As one Human Resources professional in my study noted, victims and bystanders are often hesitant to report leader toxicity. She noted that "employees should be able to go to HR, but they are not willing to put their neck on the line to take on the CEO."

Bargaining

In speaking with the survivors of toxic leadership in my study, I noted that it was common for anger and guilt to leave victims feeling vulnerable and helpless, and open for bargaining. During the bargaining stage, these survivors questioned their own actions or responses to the toxic exposure. They would wonder aloud, using phrases like, "Maybe if I just…" or "I should have ignored…" taking on blame that was not theirs to share. Catherine and I lingered in the bargaining stage for some time, attending numerous seminars. We would then exchange ideas on the ride back to the office, wondering if we could somehow use our newfound knowledge to fix Nick. When we realized this was not likely, we moved on to seminars about how to fix ourselves. We attempted to bargain with our abuser, suggesting that if we only gave more of ourselves, perhaps he would be willing to change his behaviors.

Nick was sent for anger management therapy on multiple occasions, perhaps participating in a more literal form of bargaining. Anger management, professional development, and EAP were common initial suggestions within many of my participants' organizations. However, most believed the programs to be ineffective in the end.

Depression

Depression is a difficult stage to experience. Victims of toxic leadership often find that the fight is now against themselves. In mild cases, it's a time for private mourning. But in more severe cases, survivors of toxic leadership completely withdraw from expression. If ever there was a time to extend a lifeline and reassurance, to reiterate the fact that there is hope and opportunity to come, it is during this time.

I am grateful for all who instilled in me a lifeline in the form of spiritual muscle. My community's willingness and ability to help me build resilience helped me to move quickly through this stage. I only needed a "speed date" with the depression phase, I joked after the fact. The self-esteem and support from elders in my community, including my pastor and Mr. Welcome, were key tools to building a resilience to depression.

My experience, however, is not typical. The survivors of toxic leadership I spoke with as part of my

163

study gave numerous accounts of the damage they experienced during this stage. The experience of physical ailments, work leave, and other major maladies that I discussed earlier in this book were often associated with the depression stage of processing trauma from toxic leadership. In fact, more than one of my participants chose to leave their careers, either permanently or for a long period of time.

Acceptance

Acceptance is the final and most critical stage of this grieving process. This stage is a time of reflection and realization. As important as this stage is, it is unfortunately not a happy time for many survivors, since it involves finally coming to terms with the experience of trauma and the realization that the scars of toxic leadership may last a lifetime.

This stage often requires victims to realize that they were once complicit in others' harm. Many victims also played the role of bystander, toxic follower, and some even directly victimized others. In fact, every survivor I interviewed was first a bystander to leader toxicity. Most acknowledged that their agency in preventing toxic leadership was limited by their position in the company. They felt unable to mitigate, and instead watched helplessly, observing that "good people leave good companies because of crappy managers." Many even tried to "save" the company by keeping "secrets" about the counterproductive work behaviors they saw every day. In addition to accepting their own trauma, then, the acceptance stage requires victims to accept the guilt of their complicity.

Victims must also accept, in this stage, that those who played a role in their victimization may never admit wrongdoing. I will likely never receive an apology from Nick, and I can only hope that Catherine realizes her role in his toxic abuse. While I truly believe that her contributions as a toxic follower were unintentional, they were nonetheless harmful. And yet, removing myself from the situation and beginning down my path to healing means that I no longer have contact with Catherine or Nick. It is difficult to accept that they will never face sanctions for their behavior, but doing so is an act of putting myself first. It is an act of choosing my own healing, of moving past anger and bargaining, rather than dwelling on the past harms of others.

Unfortunately, many people never reach the acceptance stage, and many victims experience these stages out of order, even sliding back and forth between the various experiences of trauma. That's okay. All trauma is unique, and therefore all roads to healing will look different. The important thing is that victims of toxic leadership are able to prioritize our own healing and, in doing so, move forward to surviving with gratefulness.

Allowing Ourselves to Heal

The road to healing looks different for all victims, just as forms of toxic leadership can take on a variety of appearances. And yet, it is important to recognize that victims of toxic leadership often leave the experience with a degree of trauma. Understanding that our victimization has left us with lasting scars is not an indication of weakness, but rather a matter of giving permission for healing.

Among my research participants, the various experiences of healing often took the shape of Kübler-Ross's stages of grieving. Experiencing these stages in different ways and in different orders, my participants reported feeling denial, anger, bargaining, depression, and acceptance about their experiences with toxic leaders, both in the role of victim and in the role of bystander or toxic follower. Understanding these stages as a normal part of the healing process allows us to be intentional and active in recovering from leader toxicity.

The good news is that, once we have processed our experiences with toxic leaders, we are better positioned to emerge from strain of workplace toxicity as survivors. This allows us to make a positive change in our workplaces, which, as I will discuss in the next chapter, is an integral part of surviving with *gratefulness*.

Chapter Five

Gratefulness

Rejoice always, pray without ceasing, in everything give thanks; for this is the will of God in Christ Jesus for you.

1 Thessalonians 5:16-18

During that difficult time when I was in the midst of toxic leadership, fearing daily for my career as well as my mental and emotional health, it was often difficult to tell what was real. Nick was a skilled manipulator, and paired with Catherine's conflict-avoidant personality, I was often gaslit into questioning my own experiences and their meaning. It was not until I had traveled some distance down the path to healing that I was able to emerge into a space of gratefulness.

Some may question how anyone could look back at an experience like mine and feel grateful. I might have questioned that myself during the ten long years of Nick's toxic abuse. But now that I have had time away, I am grateful for the perspective I have gained as a scholar of toxic leadership, and I am grateful for the ability I have, as a result of my research, to help others navigate this confusing situation.

I was recently contacted by a woman named Hope, an acquaintance who was experiencing toxicity in her workplace. She believed that the abuse she faced, including verbal aggression, passive aggressive remarks about her collegiality, and unfair performance reviews, were related to her identity as a Black woman. Her coworkers were less certain, and continually told her to "hang in there." Some of her colleagues refused to listen to her accounts of interactions with her boss at all, while others dismissed her interpretations by saying, "he's never acted like that with me."

My mind immediately rushed back to my experiences with Nick and Catherine. I was reminded of his consistent presence in my office and the way he punished others when they tried to get close to me, cutting me off from my work community. I flashed back to that terrible moment in 2016, paradoxically the worst moment of my career and the moment in which everything began moving toward my ultimate healing and gratefulness. My heart broke for her, realizing exactly what she must be feeling, and understanding as many others never will, how heavy experiences like this can weigh on your heart and soul.

I told her, "None of this is your fault. But you have the power to change it."

Together, we talked through the importance of courage, and she shared with me her sense that others in her work unit were not likely to stand up for her. We discussed strategies and approaches to resilience and persistence, brainstorming ways she could connect with communities around her to build support and spiritual muscle. I shared with her my own experience of reluctance, and cautioned her against treading water, aimlessly daydreaming about leaving the company without forming a concrete and actionable exit strategy. And finally, I asserted to her the crucial steps of healing, recommending that she find a way to speak with others who have experienced situations of toxic leaders and perhaps a professional therapist.

As I spoke with Hope, I also reflected on my own journey, and I gave myself permission to marvel at the strength I had gained through my experiences in the toxic workplace. The Bible tells us that God "forges us in the fire of struggle," refining us through life's difficulties. While I would not wish my experiences with toxic leadership on anyone, I have come to terms with what happened to me, and I am grateful for the lessons I learned as a result of Nick's abuse. And while I will always wish justice had been served and Nick had been fired from his position, I have slowly learned to let go of that anger and instead revel in my own growth. Catherine remains in her position as well, a useful if perhaps unwitting accessory to Nick's toxicity. She is a victim as well as a perpetrator, and as such, I wish her only healing and the realization of her own complicity in a structure of harm. I have chosen to unequivocally take back my own sense of control. I wish the same empowerment and strength for Hope, even though I know she may face a long road ahead.

My conversation with Hope, and others like her, drove me to seek answers. When I set out to recover from my experiences with toxic leadership, I felt alone and uncertain, as though I was feeling my way around a dark room, searching for the light switch. Then I began to conduct research on toxic leadership. Gradually, I felt the burden of isolation lifting, as participant after participant shared with me stories of our common brush with extreme toxicity. I was not alone! There is something so comforting about knowing you are in good company, and that others have successfully navigated your path and emerged feeling whole again, if sadly wiser about some of humanity's worst impulses.

My interaction with Hope was an important reminder of how lost we often feel as we attempt to navigate new, and in this case malicious, situations. Life may have prepared us to face a number of challenges, but very often toxic leadership feels beyond the scope of our emotional bandwidth. When we are in the middle of situations like this, we often feel unable to imagine what our life will look like when we finally emerge on the other side. In fact, we are often unable to imagine that we will ever emerge at all. Hope's story reminded me of that feeling, and by sharing our interaction, I hope to illustrate the importance of looking back at our experiences with a sense of gratefulness. I also hope to demonstrate that when we are grateful, we owe ourselves to work to become agents of justice for others. Gratefulness is not only about rejoicing in our own successes. It is also about doing so openly and publicly, so that others can learn from your struggles and successes.

In this chapter, I declare victory over my oppressors, celebrating my own renewed sense of self-worth and the increased strength I gained as I traveled the difficult path through toxic leadership. By celebrating what we know, and by reminding others of those discoveries, we can not only revel in our own strength and courage; we can also help to ensure that others don't face those same struggles. We can help to make the world a safer, more just place. In what follows, I aim to both give inspiration and power to those still suffering, and to offer some concrete suggestions that companies can use to prevent the development of toxic leadership in the first place.

Since much of this book is based on the premise that research-based strategies can help to prevent and respond to toxic leadership, let's begin this chapter by discussing some of the best practices for anti-toxic leadership within a particular organizational context.

Promoting Anti-Toxic Leadership

Given the horror stories of toxic leadership I have shared throughout this book, those who have not experienced life under a toxic leader may be skeptical of how such a person is hired in the first place, let alone promoted to a leadership position. We can better understand one way this happens by considering the concept of contingency leadership theory.

Let's return to the metaphor we used early in this book: that of the organization as a building. Just as there are different types of buildings, ranging perhaps from a historic weather-beaten Maine lighthouse to a towering Manhattan skyscraper shimmering in steel and glass, there are also vastly different types of organizations. Sometimes the variations are clear. Obviously a factory operates differently from a legal firm. But other variations are less transparent, and identifying and responding to these more subtle differences of organizational architecture - a business's culture, hierarchy, and personality - is the real task of leadership.

Contingency leadership theory helps us to understand the moving parts at work in leading a company through all of its unique strengths and challenges. This theory is based on the idea of situationalism, which posits that leadership means responding to the particular demands of any given situation. The ideas behind contingency leadership theory have been central to understanding the components of strong leadership since at least the early 1980s.[66] Contingency leadership theory argues that there is no universally best leadership style, since leaders must compliment the culture in which leadership is performed, the nature of the work environment, and perhaps most importantly the employees and the tasks to be accomplished. Perhaps the best-known model within the umbrella of contingency leadership theory is Hersey-Blanchard's Situational Leadership model. This model, developed in a collaboration between the California-based Center for Leadership Studies and The Ken Blanchard

178

Companies, Inc., suggests that leadership best practices depend upon leaders' ability to adjust their style based on their followers' maturity, ability, and confidence. In other words, the leader must adapt to the followers, since it is these employees who prop up the entire structure of the organization.

Returning to our building metaphor, we can imagine leadership as a maintenance crew, charged with completing all of the tasks required to maintain the integrity of the building. This would include things like daily cleaning, upkeep of electrical and plumbing systems, and replacement of any worn cosmetic elements of the building. While perhaps this all seems simple enough, recall that we have been discussing a variety of buildings. A historic, wood-framed building requires a much different type of maintenance than a steel structure. Skill in the careful process of artisanal staircase restoration does not translate well to the challenges of cleaning the windows of a chic

Manhattan skyscraper. And the harsh cleaners one might use on a modern steel and glass high-rise could be quite destructive to a two-hundred-year-old Philadelphia courthouse. While the damage might be apparent after months of this incorrect maintenance, once the corrosion was noticeable, it would be much too late to preserve the historic structure.

This is why we would be unlikely to hire someone for such a task without thoroughly vetting them. Owners of historic buildings generally take care to contract with maintenance crews skilled in restoration. They might ask for pictures of previous work, chat with the foreman about her philosophy of care toward older buildings, and speak with the crew's former clients, not only about the team's cost or profitability, but also about their experiences working with them in historical building restoration. This is precisely why leader and leadership competency models were developed with traits, behavioral skills and leader agility in mind. These models for leadership best practice can then be used to hire, train, evaluate, promote, develop, manage, and support people, taking care to match the right leaders with the right organizations.[67] As I discussed in chapter 2, techniques like emotional competency measures help to facilitate a strong initial match and ensure that applicants who pose a clear threat to the organizational architecture can be screened and removed from candidacy early in the process. Considered this way, leaders must be fitted for organizations in the same way building maintenance processes must be matched to the type of structure.

However, it is simply not enough to ensure a match between broad categories of leadership and general groups of organizations. Even the most skilled artisanal restoration specialist must do research into the trends of a particular home's construction period, the materials available at the time the building was constructed, the most accurate

material suppliers, and a host of other issues. The
maintenance crew must develop their skills, honing their
ability to match the particular building and bringing enough
flexibility to do justice to the work. This is equivalent to the
process of leadership development.

Unfortunately, while most organizations understand
the need to develop leaders, many companies fail to ensure
that leader development is linked to the organization's
strategic processes. An influential 2013 model developed
by David. L. Dinwoodie of the Center for Creative
Leadership identified four elements that must be core to an
effective and situationally responsive leader.[68] First, leaders
must be forward thinking enough to anticipate the way
business changes will impact the culture of the
organization. Second, leaders should be skilled at shaping
the organizational culture in a way that makes all
individuals feel safe and welcome. Third, leaders must seek
out approaches that balance apparently polarized

organizational goals, finding ways to bring together things like increases in profitability and maintenance of employee benefits. And finally, leaders should develop ways of encouraging collaboration, breaking down barriers between apparently distinct groups of employees and incentivizing synergy between independent teams.

The purpose of the Dinwoodie model is not simply to develop better leaders. More specifically, the Center for Creative Leadership encourages leadership development *in alignment with the organization's strategic process.* In other words, by laying out four core elements of leadership that require analysis of a particular organizational setting, this model demands that leaders be developed situationally. As Dinwoodie clarifies in a 2014 white paper, the central aim of this process is not only to build effective leaders, but to ensure that the organizational culture is functional and healthy. Companies that neglect the maintenance of their organizational culture and, as an extension their leadership culture, are likely to find themselves struggling to achieve core business strategies as well.[69] In other words, organizational culture is not separate from leadership style, and these two components work together to dictate the overall success of the business.

An ethical approach to non-toxic leadership development also includes regular measurement processes. In the experiences of my participants, as well as my own struggle under toxic leadership, toxic leadership could have easily been stopped if the company had implemented processes of leadership assessment with an eye toward ethical organizational values. You can't manage what you can't measure, and any company invested in maintaining a healthy organizational culture must put into place mechanisms for feedback. In a 2014 review of best practices for leadership development, experts from the University of Western Australia, the Center for Creative Leadership, and the University of Houston highlight one solution to this challenge: the Multisource Performance Appraisal.[70] Also known as 360-degree feedback or multisource feedback, this performance measurement appraisal tool offers a structure for soliciting feedback from an individual's supervisor, peers, and subordinates, as well as the person being evaluated themself. The administration of multiple levels and interventions of feedback improves the effectiveness more than a single level or intervention, and can prove an early detector of toxic leader's behaviors.

Multisource Performance Appraisals are widely accepted and used by US Human Resources Managers to reinforce positive changes in leader behavior and to provide leaders with a concrete mechanism for self-reflection and self-development.[71] Additionally, this tool is an effective way to promote continuous leadership development, a positive for both organizational culture and institutional higher-ups interested in promoting their proactive growth strategies. Multisource Performance Appraisals can even be used to directly educate leaders on the emotional and financial effects of toxic behaviors on workers and the institutions. However, given that research on Multisource Performance Appraisals consistently suggests that leaders only grow and change when they are invested in doing so, this type of assessment tool must be used in conjunction with screening mechanisms to prevent the hiring and promotion of toxic leaders in the first place.[72]

There's a plethora of reasons that businesses should intentionally screen for the traits that lead to toxic leadership, including narcissism, authoritarianism, and abusive behaviors. But avoiding the hiring and promotion of individuals who already display the tendencies of toxicity in the workplace is not enough. Corporations who are serious about promoting a healthy and productive workplace environment must also take care to develop and assess their leaders. And, to be clear, any organization interested in financial profitability and long-term success should be invested in these important components of workplace culture. To ignore the presence of toxicity in leadership culture is to open the door to a range of expensive issues from frequent employee turnover, the costs of increased medical and personal leave, the loss of productivity from employees who withdraw and mentally check out, and even lawsuits and settlements when employees suffer under toxic leaders.

Just as it is important for individuals who have experienced toxic leadership to heal and grow into a sense of gratefulness and strength, it is also key for organizations to recognize patterns of toxicity in today's corporate environment. One way to take seriously the threat of corporate leadership toxicity is to understand the general recommendations from Human Resources Managers who have dealt with toxic leaders in their day-to-day working lives.

Human Resources as Anti-Toxin

Achieving true gratefulness is not only about understanding toxic situations. It is also about taking action to help stop toxicity from forming in the first place, and stepping up to prevent others from suffering in the ways we have. If we want to survive toxic leadership with gratefulness, we must continue to heal until we finally feel liberated enough to share our strength and courage with others. True gratefulness, I believe, requires that we imagine a new, more just workplace environment that uses best practices to intervene in toxic leadership before it has an opportunity to thrive.

Among the most consistent findings of my research was the clear knowledge of toxicity from Human Resources Managers. Employees always know of their own experiences with toxicity, and perhaps their trusted colleagues or cliques understand their shared experiences as well. But nearly across the board, it is the local-level

Human Resources Manager who best understands the variation and complexity of a leader's toxic behaviors. It is therefore Human Resources Managers, particularly those positioned within the workplace, who are best equipped to function as an anti-toxin, supporting and being supported by corporate strategies for ethical and healthy workplace behavior. As the many site-based Human Resources Managers told me, they are well positioned to function as a tool for corporate anti-toxicity programs at the crucial levels identified by previous research including screening, development, and assessment. Moreover, my research revealed a final step that was neglected in a surprising number of cases: follow-through.

Screening

Site-level Human Resources Managers play a key role in screening potential managers, both in the case of new hires and promotions. As I spoke with participants, I noticed that a very small set of them were using the

Predictive Index as a tool. These participants cited this measurement as a way they had successfully predicted both leadership toxicity and general leadership ineffectiveness in the past, and were the only two Human Resources professionals who truly appeared to have a handle on proactively mitigating leader toxicity.

The Predictive Index is a behavioral measurement tool used by Human Resources to measure work skills and behavior. Employers use the tool for leader development, executive on-boarding, and team building efforts. The Predictive Index is backed by research, studies, and psychologists. Participants in this study reported success in using the tool to better understand their managers and C-suite executive leadership styles, strengths and qualities. This mechanism of psychometric assessment was developed in the early 1940s by military veteran Arnold Daniels, and it has since grown into a rigorously tested best practice for predicting leadership behaviors prior to hiring and internal leadership promotion.

In an unusually positive interview, Stephen told me that this company held firm to their use of Predictive Index, and rigorously followed a series of screening procedures based in best practice. Stephen's company is truly a model for how this type of screening would be done. For Stephen, hiring includes a

> Rigorous interview process that requires the approval of the direct supervisor and the potential leader's two up supervisor. As an example, if the CFO is hiring a leader, he must approve via interview and the CEO must approve via interview. In all leadership decisions a final interview is held with me, [the Chief Human Resources Officer]. My interview is based on our three pillars of leadership: character, managerial courage, and execution. If at

the end of my interview, I do not believe they

possess the three pillars, we do not hire them.

Key to the success of this process is the alignment of the

screening process with the company's clear strategic plan,

as well as the empowerment of the Human Resources

officer to make a final decision on fit.

Development
However, in the case of internal promotion, often

screenings are seen as irrelevant. This is far from the case,

as Dianna's company makes clear. She noted that her

company had good intentions, but when it came to

promoting from within, the organization often fell short in

actively following their own screening guidelines. As she

noted:

> Generally, I believe that we try to select the "right"
>
> people for promotions. Often, organizations select
>
> great individual contributors to lead people but fail
>
> to identify the characteristics of those that have the

right leadership qualities that are most likely to
bring out the best in others.

Dianna's complaint is unfortunately common, and reflects a
tendency for corporate promotional decisions to be based
exclusively on past performance rather than future promise.
In many cases, Dianna emphasized, this type of focus leads
to individuals being promoted one step beyond their
competency levels, a situation colloquially referred to as
"the Peter principle."

The Human Resources Managers in Dianna's
company had trained upper management personnel in
screening for potential toxicity. However, Human
Resources themselves were not given the opportunity to
actively filter candidates for promotion. Since many leaders
are chosen from within the company, the area of leadership
development is a key opening for the introduction of
toxicity.

Assessment

Although every participant I spoke with strongly advocated for Multisource Feedback during performance evaluations, most believed that their organization's leadership would be resistant to the idea. In many cases, participants shared that performance evaluations were utilized only to monitor lower-level employees, and that leaders at all levels seemed exempt from this type of review. As the stories throughout this book should demonstrate, this is a grave error that leaves toxic leaders unchecked, and, as a result, sets companies up for a range of issues ranging from legal liability to dramatic decreases in employee motivation and productivity.

In fact, even with assessment protocols in place, toxic leadership grows so quickly, it can begin to wreak havoc even between annual performance reviews. Niles shared an instance of this type of rapid escalation. Although his company did not have a formal Multisource Feedback protocol in place, he had implemented weekly meetings with staff to monitor the experiences of the organization's employees. In at least one instance, Niles shared, a toxic leader became apparent even before extreme behaviors could be identified; the leader's toxicity showed itself not through gossip and high turnover, but through "an increase in work related injuries in employees." Since Niles was aware of the issues of toxic leadership, and since he was paying close attention to trends in his organization, he was able to quickly identify the toxic leader at the root of this negative trend.

Follow-Through

However, identifying toxic leaders is only valuable, Niles emphasized, if upper management believes that toxic leadership is a "real thing," something that was not the case at his organization. Of all the issues raised to me by participants, the indifference of executives to toxic leadership was the most consistently disappointing. Rooting out toxic leaders through screening, development, and assessment is only effective if leaders are willing to follow through, actually removing the toxic leader from the position.

The lack of action on the part of upper management had left Jada cynical and frustrated. In an account that reminded me very much of my own experiences with Nick and Catherine, she told me,

> Not enough ever happens. That's the raw truth. They are sent to training and classes and spoken to "off the record." But they never change. And their victims continue to suffer. Then people quit. That's it. Those are the consequences. Good people quit good companies because of crappy managers. Then the whole company suffers the loss of those good employees.

For Jada, the most difficult part was the clarity with which she could predict the outcome of leader toxicity, while also being rendered helpless by upper management. As a dedicated Human Resources representative, Jada told me about her many efforts, writing "handbooks and numerous policies," but without the backing of highly ranked executives, she was unable to intervene for the employees she was charged with supporting. And yet, her perspective on the situation was clear and guided by best practices along with over a decade of experience watching the stark differences in morale, productivity, and general workplace attitude under a toxic leader as opposed to a strong, healthy leadership model. "There should not be any room in business for a toxic leader," she stated firmly. "This is an oxymoron. You cannot be toxic and a leader. That is fear driving – not leading."

As I have argued throughout this book, toxic leadership is only enabled by particular structural choices within organizational architecture and culture. These four moments - screening, development, assessment, and follow-through - are consistent points of entry for toxicity in an organization, or the crucial maintenance that prevents the organization's erosion. If the owner of a building allowed its foundation to rot, its structural support beams to rust, or its drywall to grow mold, we would consider that owner to be negligent. This lack of action physically endangers anyone who frequents the building, and sets up that owner for legal action and a loss of the property's functionality. The same is true of organizations that allow weaknesses in structure to create vulnerabilities for their employees. By implementing research-based best practices that protect the organization at each of these key moments, organizational leadership can shore up the architecture of their company, preventing the emotional turmoil, medical liability, and financial losses that accompany toxic leaders.

An Apology Isn't Enough

When we experience harm, we often appreciate and deserve a heartfelt apology. However, an apology without a change in behavior is meaningless. If our abusers do not stop their traumatizing behavior, an apology becomes a device for continued oppression rather than a tool for healing. To truly survive toxic leadership with gratefulness, we need more than words; we need actions. Previous research has given us a plethora of tools that can be used to eliminate toxic leadership. Psychological screening tools and multilevel performance assessments offer ways of preventing toxic leaders from being hired and promoted and, when that fails, identifying it as it unfolds within our companies. However, while some of those actions can be achieved by Human Resources managers and other employees, many require the investments of upper-level management. To truly conquer toxic leadership, we must advocate for research-based solutions in our organizations not only at the ground levels, but all the way to the top of the corporate food chain. Eliminating the emotionally, physically, and financially expensive problem of toxic leadership requires buy-in at all levels of an organizational structure.

In this chapter, I discussed the role of gratefulness in truly healing and moving forward from toxic leadership. This last step completes the process at the heart of this book. The final pages of this book will be dedicated to synthesizing the process of surviving toxic leadership with gratefulness. As I conclude, I will review the components of this process and offer concrete solutions for those dealing with toxic leadership now as well as those who aim to prevent it in the future.

Conclusion

In this book, I shared personal and chilling accounts of my nearly ten-year experience with a toxic leader, along with lived experiences of Human Resources professionals that I collected during my research on leadership toxicity. I no longer consider myself a victim, but a survivor. I survived toxic leadership with gratefulness.

Ultimately, the task of addressing toxicity in the workplace should be an organizational goal. It should include high-level leadership, Human Resources professionals who are tasked with handling toxic situations, and the workers who comprise an organization's architecture and culture through their daily routines. Detecting and counteracting organizational toxicity will help mitigate the damage to employees, organizations, and other stakeholders. This book is therefore a call for both justice and action.

It is my hope that this book is used as a resource for mitigating toxic leadership. I hope victims of leader toxicity, who consistently endure the overbearing weight of this daunting experience, find solace in the book. But, moreover, I hope this book helps to make the workplace a safer, more just place where others don't face the struggles I have described.

SURVIVING TOXIC LEADERSHIP WITH GRATEFULNESS

If you are a victim of leader toxicity, I hope this book has helped you to learn more about the structures at work in your abuse. I hope it has motivated you to practice self-care and to be courageous to make healthy decisions about your next steps, whether those include seeking a support group, consulting a counselor, journaling about the experience, or other approaches to healing from trauma. Do what it takes to keep your mind at peace.

If toxic leadership is not something you have experienced directly, but something you have the power to help prevent and solve, this book can function as a resource for advocacy. Use the stories and scholarship included in this book to build courage in yourself and others. Move forward with the concrete solutions I have discussed in these pages, and help others to realize that they are not alone, and that toxic leadership is a dangerous threat to individual and organizational health and well-being.

Dr. Margaret E. Gary

As both a survivor and an advocate, I understand how difficult it can be to face feelings of self-doubt. I struggled to truly see my experience as a real trauma, and as a result, I put off healing for longer than necessary. It was my research on toxic leadership that finally helped me to face my feelings. During the process of conducting the study that formed the basis of this book, I learned, without a doubt, that leader toxicity is a widespread issue. Faced with so many others who had experienced situations like mine, I felt armed with evidence confirming that my situation was real. I was not alone. I knew I needed to share my findings with others, educating victims on the underling structures and systems at work in leader toxicity. And allowing victims to realize, as I did, that they are not alone. My goal was to go beyond simply identifying toxic leaders - research on the definitions and characteristics of toxic leaders are plentiful, and those who have experienced it know it well. In my research I clearly saw that toxic leadership is not the problem of one, rogue abuser. Toxic leadership is a structural, systemic issue. The web of toxicity extends outwards from the leader, making it important to identify the behaviors of bystanders and victims that support leader toxicity. I provided critical antidotes such as *courage and perseverance*, revealed the harmful habits that characterize *reluctance*, and offered life changing steps such as *healing* and *gratefulness* to combat leader toxicity.

A great deal of **courage** on the part of organizations, bystanders (most notably, Human Resources professionals), and victims is necessary to mitigate toxic leadership. My research unexpectedly revealed that HR professionals are often victims, or collateral damage, of toxic leadership. Yet, this does not negate their professional responsibilities to intervene, rather than remain complicit, in leader toxicity. Being courageous is not always easy.

But, failing to be courageous can be detrimental to both victim and bystander as well as the organization as a whole.

It is important to realize both the power and pause in community, work and otherwise. Positive communities are key to **perseverance** and resilience, and the strength they provide are crucial to overcoming obstacles and adversity. Things like self-esteem built during childhood, church affiliation, or honest and authentic work relationships all help to build what my pastor, Dr. Tolbert, calls spiritual muscle. On the contrary, recall that communities can be affected by the emotional failures or abuses of leader toxicity, tearing down their own members rather than building them up.

These negative effects lead to **reluctance,** a very dangerous and costly space many victims and bystanders occupy. Reluctant to take action, many victims of toxic leadership fail to quit in the traditional fashion. Instead, they may simply disengage, compromising the social and economic health of the organization and individuals within

it. Organizations, Human Resources professionals,

employees, and even leaders must recognize the part they

play in reluctance and help to intervene before reluctance

takes its toll on the entire workplace.

While time does not heal all wounds, time used

efficiently can heal wounds. **Healing** requires an

acknowledgement and release of negative behaviors and

feelings that weigh us down. To do so, victims must gain

sufficient understanding of the source of their pain. We

don't all heal in the same ways, so each person who has

experienced the trauma of toxic leadership must discover

the healing path that is best for them. Healing turns victims

into survivors, and allows us to take back the power from

our oppressors.

Achieving true **gratefulness** is not only about

understanding toxic situations. It is also about taking action

to prevent leader toxicity and stepping up to prevent others from suffering. Organizations must build a solid architecture and culture resistant to toxicity. Included in this architecture and culture must be a competent and empowered Human Resources system that serves as an anti-toxin. Finally, rejoice and be grateful. Declare victory over your oppressor. You are no longer a victim; you are a survivor! Revel in your newfound strength, courage, and peace.

Supporting Anti-Toxic Architecture

The foundation of *Surviving Toxic Leadership with Gratefulness* is made up of the stories that were generously shared with me by professionals who participated in my phenomenological study. These stories, featured throughout this book, provide four overarching correctives to mitigate toxic leadership. These actionable items include *recognizing the costs of toxic leadership, removing toxic leaders, taking preventative measures,* and *supporting Human Resources professionals at the organizational level.*

Recognizing the Costs of Toxic Leadership

Leaders are linked to organizational effectiveness

and employee performance.[73] The toxic leaders identified

in my research consistently displayed self-centered,

dysfunctional, and destructive characteristics. These leaders

engaged in behaviors that included dishonesty, arrogance,

intimidation, and demoralizing and undermining tactics that

cause serious and enduring harm to organizations,

individuals, and other stakeholders. All participants

identified turnover, diminished morale, loss of productivity,

disruption of business, and reduced job satisfaction as

among the most severe costs of toxic leadership. Each of

these damages emerge in the costly forms of employee

reluctance.

Removing Toxic Leaders

Toxic leadership negatively affects an

organization's culture. As a consequence, organizational

cultures become infused with toxicity that leads to a host of

individual and organizational problems. My participants

recognized this, and urged others in Human Resources as in their own organizations to acknowledge the real and pervasive threat of toxic leadership. For my participants, this meant taking an unequivocal stand against toxic leaders and removing them from their positions. This takes courage. In fact, most participants in this study believed training is not affective, restoring trust is difficult, and retaliation from the toxic leader, after disciplinary actions, is highly likely. Therefore, while I acknowledge the position of previous research that suggests that disciplinary action may be enough, I advocate instead for removal.[74]

Taking Preventative Measures

It has been well-documented that there are behaviors that indicate a potential for a leader to become a toxic leader.[75] However, most of the professionals who participated in my study stated that organizations are not proactive in mitigating leader toxicity. Speaking from their combined years of experience, these professionals suggested that organizations rarely implement tools such as

formal prescreening, Human Resources and leadership

training specific to toxic leadership, and transparency in the

performance management of leaders. In response, all of my

participants advocated for the widespread use of

prescreening, training, and performance management with

follow-up protocols.

Supporting Human Resources Professionals at the Organizational Level

Human Resources professionals face limitations in

their ability to prevent and eliminate toxic leadership.

Factors like organizational incompetency and the dismissal

of Human Resources recommendations can severely

constrain the ability of these professionals to protect

workers from toxic leadership. Most participants perceived

that complaints against toxic leaders are generally ignored,

particularly when the predator was in a high-power position

like CEO, Vice President, or Director. The participants in

this study felt strongly that they have been entrusted with

the responsibility to mitigate leader toxicity, but that their organizations failed to give them the authority to do so. This was reported to be especially prevalent when the predator was in a high-power position.

Taken together, these findings offer a platform for advocacy. Throughout this book, I have written in depth about the specific ways these findings emerged in my study, and those who find the courage to work against toxic leadership should lean on the stories of participants and the previous research detailed in earlier chapters. By embracing these four action items, organizations can protect themselves against the harms of toxic leadership, whether they are interested in the financial bottom-line, the health of their workers, or, ideally, both.

Supporting Victims and Survivor

Throughout this book, I made numerous references to the fact that toxic leadership affects individuals, organizations, and all stakeholders. I noted that

organizations are often reactive to the damage caused by

toxicity, rather than taking a proactive, preventative stance.

Toxic leadership has received widespread recognition over

the last decade, demonstrating a need for actionable

solutions and preventative training on leader toxicity in

business, management, leadership, and Human Resources

training courses. Until that time, individuals must take

action against workplace toxicity and support those who

have suffered at the hands of a toxic leader. This includes

raising awareness of antecedents of the toxic behavior, the

remnants left behind after exposure, and the urgent need for

self-care across our society.

The first step in transforming from victim to

survivor is realizing that you have experienced trauma.

Often this requires learning about the structures and

systems of oppression, and I hope that this book is a useful tool for understanding the contours of toxic leadership as they are reflected in your own experiences.

Once we realize that our trauma *is* trauma, we can begin a variety of actions to begin the healing process. Throughout the healing process and beyond, we can embrace a variety of self-care practices. These may include yoga, stretching, and breathing techniques, as well as a variety of holistic approaches. I personally found solace in journaling. Writing down your thoughts and feelings can help bring clarity to your experience. Think back to your childhood diary, where you were able to disclose emotions, fun, fears, and struggles. This was affective because it allowed for self-discovery without outside judgement or punishment.

However, as you write in your journal, you may find yourself making discoveries that you are not prepared to process. In this case, you may need to seek someone with the skills to support trauma recovery. Be in tune with your healing and know when to seek outside help or

professional therapy. There is no shame in seeking out

help, and in fact, you may find that working with a

professional helps you to shed internalized shame that

remains from your experiences of abuse.

In addition to professional counseling, you may find

it helpful to seek out others who share your experience. As

I moved through my own experiences as well as this

research, I was surprised to learn there are various support

groups for survivors of toxic leadership. If you are not able

to locate one near you, consider starting one. This is an

excellent way to embrace your gratefulness as a survivor,

as it allows you to transform your toxic experience into a

foundation for supporting others.

Overall, remember that you are not alone. The

accounts of toxic leadership in this book are only the tip of

the iceberg. Unfortunately, toxic leadership is a widespread

problem. Embrace the community of survivors and take

comfort in the growing movement to end toxic leadership once and for all.

March Forth and Do Great Things

On my last day at the company, I walked into my office, turned on the light, placed my purse on the desk, and looked around the office I'd occupied for nearly two decades. I felt a little anxious, as I wasn't sure what the next day would bring. Minutes later, one of the workers I supervised appeared in my doorway holding a "thank you" card. The card read "March 4th (forth) and do great things!"

After seeing the perplexed look on my face, he asked, "Was it on purpose or a coincidence that your last day is March 4th?"

I looked at the calendar with surprise. Grinning, I replied, "No, it wasn't on purpose, but it certainly isn't a coincidence."

Of all the things in my life that I've managed to defeat, I have not been able to defeat time. The dilemma is that God appoints and controls each season in the cycle of

life. As Ecclesiastes 3:1-8 explains,

> There is a time for everything, and a season for
>
> every activity under heaven: a time to be born and a
>
> time to die, a time to plant and a time to uproot, a
>
> time to kill and a time to heal, a time to tear down
>
> and a time to build, a time to weep and a time to
>
> laugh, a time to mourn and a time to dance, a time
>
> to scatter stones and a time to gather them, a time to
>
> embrace and a time to refrain, a time to search and a
>
> time to give up, a time to keep and a time to throw
>
> away, a time to tear and a time to mend, a time to be
>
> silent and a time to speak, a time to love and a time
>
> to hate, a time for war and a time for peace.

This card from my supervisee was confirmation that I'd

made the right decision. That my time for peace and new

opportunities had come. While I knew the road to recovery

may be a challenge, I suddenly felt confident that I would

be okay. And I knew I wasn't alone. Still not having a clue what my next move would be, I took a deep breath, then exhaled. I felt an incredible sense of relief and gratefulness wash over me.

I hope that you, too, will march forth and find the courage to survive with gratefulness.

ABOUT THE AUTHOR

 Dr. Margaret E. Gary is a business leader and entrepreneur who has lead teams and projects for more than 20 years. She previously earned a master's in business administration with a specialization of healthcare management and a bachelor's in psychology at Saint Leo University. Dr. Gary's professional experience includes college professor, human resources and staff development manager, CS & international B2B and B2C sales manager, where her responsibilities included marketing, operations, accounting, and finance management. Dr. Gary is the diversity chair of HR Florida State Council's Ocala chapter, with past board responsibilities of workforce readiness chair. She is passionate about children, therefore much of her volunteer efforts are focused in child advocacy. She serves as a board member at Children Home Society, volunteers for Academic Year in America, and volunteers for Junior Achievement U.S.A.

Endnotes

1. See for example Anjum, A., Yasmeen, K., & Yasmeen, K. (2011). Bullying at work: A comprehensive definition and consequences based on an empirical study. *International Journal of Human Resource Studies*, *1*(1), 80-88; Goldman, A. (2006). High toxicity leadership: Borderline personality disorder and the dysfunctional organization. *Journal of Managerial Psychology*, *21*(8), 733-746; Einarsen, S., Hoel, H., & Cooper, C. (Eds.). (2003). *Bullying and emotional abuse in the workplace: International perspectives in research and practice.* Boca Raton, Florida: CRC Press.

2. ibid.

3. See for example, Carlock, D. H. (2013). *Beyond bullying: A holistic exploration of the organizational toxicity phenomenon* (Order No. 3556871). Available from ProQuest Dissertations & Theses A&I. (1328403875);

Lipman-Blumen, J. (2006). *The allure of toxic leaders: Why we follow destructive bosses and corrupt politicians- and how we can survive them.* New York: Oxford University Press Inc.

4. ibid., Maxwell, S. M. (2015). *An Exploration of Human Resource Personnel and Toxic Leadership* (Doctoral dissertation, Walden University). Retrieved from https://works.bepress.com/sabrina_maxwell/1/

5. Whicker, M. L. (1996). *Toxic leaders: When organizations go bad.* Westport, CT: Quorum Books.

6. Schmidt, A. A. (2008). *Development and validation of the toxic leadership scale.* (Master's thesis). Available from ProQuest Dissertations and Theses database.

7. Padilla, A., Hogan, R., & Kaiser, R. B. (2007). The toxic triangle: Destructive leaders, susceptible followers, and conducive environments. *The Leadership Quarterly, 18(3), 176-194.*

8. Reed, G. E. (2004). Toxic leadership. *Military Review, 84*(4), 67.

9. Wang, H., Sui, Y., Luthans, F., Wang, D., & Wu, Y. (2014). Impact of authentic leadership on performance: Role of followers' positive psychological capital and relational processes. Journal of Organizational Behavior. 35(1), 5-21.

10. Cohen, T. R., Panter, A. T., & Turan, N. (2013). Predicting counterproductive work behavior from guilt proneness. *Journal of Business Ethics, 114*(1), 45-53.

11. Jensen, J. M., & Patel, P. C. (2011). Predicting counterproductive work behavior from the interaction of personality traits. *Personality and Individual Differences,*

51(4), 466-471.

12. Hogan, S. J., & Coote, L. V. (2014). Organizational culture, innovation, and performance: A test of Schein's model. *Journal of Business Research, 67*(8), 1609-1621; Naranjo Valencia, J.,C., Raquel, S. V., & Daniel Jiménez Jiménez. (2010). Organizational culture as determinant of product innovation. *European Journal of Innovation Management, 13*(4), 466-480.doi:http://dx.doi.org/10.1108/14601061011086294.

13. Carroll, A., & Buchholtz, A. (2014). *Business and society: Ethics, sustainability, and stakeholder management.* Mason, Ohio: Cengage Learning; Day, D. V. (2001). Leadership development: A review in context. *The Leadership Quarterly, 11*(4), 581-613; Du Plessis, A., & Sukumaran, S. (2015). The Role of HRM in Leadership Development, Talent Retention, Knowledge Management, and Employee Engagement. *World, 5*(1).

14. García-Morales, V. J., Jiménez-Barrionuevo, M. M., & Gutiérrez-Gutiérrez, L. (2012). Transformational leadership influence on organizational performance through organizational learning and innovation. *Journal of Business Research,* 65(7),1040-1050; Rothaermel, F. T. (2014). *Strategic management: Concepts and cases (2nd ed.).* New York: McGraw-Hill Irwin.

15. Dinwoodie, D. L., Quinn, L., & McGuire, J. B. (2014). *Bridging the Strategy/Performance Gap How Leadership Strategy Drives Business Results,* p. 2.

16. Day (2001). Leadership development.

17. Schmidt (2008) *Development and validation of the toxic leadership scale.*

18. Campion, M. A., Fink, A. A., Ruggeberg, B. J., Carr, L., Phillips, G. M., & Odman, R. B. (2011). Doing competencies well: Best practices in competency modeling. *Personnel Psychology,* 64(1), 225-262.

19. Boddy, C. R. (2015). Psychopathic leadership a case study of a corporate psychopath CEO. *Journal of Business Ethics*, 1-16; Shaw, J. B., Erickson, A., & Nassirzadeh, F. (2014). Destructive leader behaviour: A study of Iranian leaders using the destructive leadership Questionnaire. *Leadership, 10*(2), 218-239.

20. Carroll & Buchholtz (2014). *Business and society.*

21. Barling, J., Slater, F., & Kevin Kelloway, E. (2000). Transformational leadership and emotional intelligence: An exploratory study. *Leadership & Organization Development Journal, 21*(3), 157-161; Goleman, D., Boyatzis, R., & McKee, A. (2001). Primal leadership: The hidden driver of great performance. *Harvard Business Review, 79*(11), 42-53.

22. Stevens, W. (2010). *Using emotional intelligence as a leadership strategy to make good leaders great* (Order No. 3569338). Available from ProQuest Dissertations & Theses A&I. (1353613809). Retrieved from http:search.proquest.com.ezprozy. saintleo.edu/docview/1353613809?accountid=4870

23. Neumann, R., & Strack, F. (2000). Mood contagion: The automatic transfer of mood between persons. *Journal of personality and social psychology, 79*(2), 211.

24. Stevens (2010). *Using emotional intelligence as a leadership strategy to make good leaders great.*

25. Goleman, et al. (2001). Primal leadership.

26. Whicker (1996). *Toxic leaders.*

27. Appelbaum, S. H., & Roy-Girard, D. (2007). Toxins in the workplace: Effect on organizations and employees. *Corporate Governance: The International Journal of Business in Society, 7*(1), 17-28; Carlock (2013). *Beyond bullying*; Lipman-Blumen (2006). *The allure of toxic leaders*; Maxwell (2015). *An Exploration of Human*

Resource Personnel and Toxic Leadership; Whicker (1996). *Toxic leaders.*

28. Stevens (2010). *Using emotional intelligence as a leadership strategy to make good leaders great.*

29. Maxwell (2015). *An Exploration of Human Resource Personnel and Toxic Leadership,* p. 3.

30. Goleman et al. (2001), Primal leadership.

31. ibid., p. 44.

32. García-Morales et al (2012), Transformational leadership influence on organizational performance through organizational learning and innovation; Rothaermel (2014), *Strategic management.*

33. Lipman-Blumen (2006), *The allure of toxic leaders.*

34. Schaubroeck, J., Walumbwa, F. O., Ganster, D. C., & Kepes, S. (2007). Destructive leader traits and the neutralizing influence of an "enriched" job. *The Leadership Quarterly, 18*(3), 236-251.

35. Webster, V., Brough, P., & Daly, K. (2014). Fight, flight or freeze: Common responses for follower coping with toxic leadership. *Stress and Health.* John Wiley & Sons, Ltd. DOI: 10.1002/smi.2626.

36. Schaubroek et al (2007), Destructive leader traits and the neutralizing influence of an "enriched" job.

37. Webster et al (2014), Fight, flight or freeze: Common responses for follower coping with toxic leadership.

38. Lipman-Blumen (2006), *The allure of toxic leaders.*

39. Webster et al (2014), Fight, flight or freeze: Common responses for follower coping with toxic leadership.

40. Cowan, R. L. (2009). *Walking the tightrope: Workplace bullying and the human resource professional*

(Doctoral dissertation, Texas A&M University). Retrieved from http://oaktrust.library.tamu.edu/bitstream/handle/1969.1/ET D-TAMU-2009-12-7497/COWAN-DISSERTATION.pdf?sequence=2

41. ibid.

42. Kehoe, R. R., & Wright, P. M. (2013). The impact of high-performance human resource practices on employees' attitudes and behaviors. *Journal of Management, 39*(2), 366-391; Marks, M. L., & Mirvis, P. H. (2011). A framework for the human resources role in managing culture in mergers and acquisitions. *Human Resource Management,* 50(6), 859-877.

43. Rynes, S. L., Colbert, A. E., & Brown, K. G. (2002). HR professionals' beliefs about effective human resource practices: Correspondence between research and practice. *Human Resource Management, 41*(2), 149-174.

44. ibid, 164.

45. ibid.

46. Wright, P. M., McMahan, G. C., & McWilliams, A. (1994). Human resources and sustained competitive advantage: a resource-based perspective. *International journal of human resource management, 5*(2), 301-326.

47. Hollis, L. P. (2015). Bully university? The cost of workplace bullying and employee disengagement in American Higher Education. *Sage Open.* DOI: 10.1177/2158244015589997, p. 1.

48. Robinson, B. (2019). Two-thirds of workers experienced burnout this year: How to reverse the trend in 2020. *Forbes.* Retrieved from https://www.forbes.com/sites/bryanrobinson/2019/12/08/two-thirds-of-workers-experienced-burnout-this-year-how-to-reverse-the-trend-in-2020/?sh=32167a837974

49. Alexander, J. C., Eyerman, R., Giesen, B., Smelter, N. J., Sztompka, P. (2004). *Cultural trauma and collective identity.* Berkeley: University of California Press.
50. ibid., p. 7
51. Casper, M. J. & Wertheimer, E. (2016), *Critical trauma studies: Understanding violence, conflict, and memory in everyday life.* New York: New York University Press.
52. Alexander, et al. (2004), *Cultural trauma and collective identity.*
53. Buhle, J.T.,
J.A. Silvers, T.D. Wager, R. Lopez, C. Onyemekwu, H. K ober, J. Weber, K.N. Ochsner (2014). Cognitive reappraisal of emotion: a meta-analysis of human neuroimaging studies. *Cereb. Cortex., 24,* 2981-2990, 10.1093/cercor/bht154.
54. Lazarus, R. S. (1966). *Psychological stress and the coping process.* McGraw-Hill.
55. Friendlander, S. (1979). *When memory comes.* New York: Farrar, Strauss, and Giroux.
56. Van der Kolk, B. (2014). *The body keeps the score: Brain, mind, and body in the healing of trauma.* New York: Penguin Random House.
57. McAvoy, B. R., & Murtagh, J. (2003). *Workplace bullying: The silent epidemic.*
58. McAvoy & Murtagh (2003), *Workplace bullying.*
59. Moore, S. A., Zoellner, L. A., & Mollenholt, N. (2008). Are expressive suppression and cognitive reappraisal associated with stress-related symptoms?. *Behaviour research and therapy, 46*(9), 993-1000.
60. Lanius, R. A., Hopper, J. W., & Menon, R. S. (2003). Individual differences in a husband and wife who developed PTSD after a motor vehicle accident: a

functional MRI case study. *American Journal of Psychiatry, 160*(4), 667-669.

61. Namie, G. (2014). Workplace bullying survey. *Workplace Bullying Institute.* Retrieved from https://icos.umich.edu/sites/default/files/lecturereadinglists/ WBI-2014-US-Survey.print_.pdf

62. ibid.

63. Attell, B. K., Brown, K. K., & Trieber, L. (2017), Workplace bullying, perceived job stressors, and psychological distress: Gender and race differences in the stress process. *Social Science Research,* 65. Doi: 10.1016/j.ssresearch.2017.02.001.

64. ibid.

65. Moore, et al (2008), Are expression suppression and cognitive reappraisal associated with stress-related symptoms?

66. Hersey, P, Blanchard, KH. Grid® principles and situationalism: both! a response to blake and mouton. Group Organ Stud 1982; 7(2): 207–210.

67. (Campion et al. (2011), Doing competencies well; Derue, D. S., Nahrgang, J. D., Wellman, N. E. D., & Humphrey, S. E. (2011). Trait and behavioral theories of leadership: An integration and meta-analytic test of their relative validity. *Personnel psychology, 64*(1), 7-52; Dinh, J. E., Lord, R. G., Gardner, W. L., Meuser, J. D., Liden, R. C., & Hu, J. (2014). Leadership theory and research in the new millennium: Current theoretical trends and changing perspectives. *The Leadership Quarterly, 25*(1), 36-62; Schaubroeck et al., (2007), Destructive leader traits and the neutralizing influence of an "enriched" job.

68. Dinwoodie, D.L. (2013). *Strategic Leadership Challenges: Findings of Empirical Data Analysis.* Greensboro, NC: Center for Creative Leadership.

69. ibid.

70. Day, D. V., Fleenor, J. W., Atwater, L. E., Sturm, R. E., & McKee, R. A. (2014), Advances in leader and leadership development: A review of 25 years of research and theory, *The Leadership Quarterly*, 25 (1): 63-82.

71. Atwater, L. E., Brett, J. F., & Charles, A. C. (2007). Multisource feedback: Lessons learned and implications for practice. *Human Resource Management*, *46*(2), 285-307; Ermongkonchai, P. (2008). An evaluation of multisource feedback (MSF) for managerial development in large-size manufacturing companies in Thailand. *Contemporary Management Research*, *4*(3); Campbell, J., Narayanan, A., Burford, B., & Greco, M. (2010). Validation of a multi-source feedback tool for use in general practice. *Education for Primary Care*, *21*(3), 165-179.

72. Atwater, Brett, & Charles (2007), Multisource feedback.

73. García-Morales et al (2012), Transformational leadership influence on organizational performance through organizational learning and innovation; Rothaermel (2014), *Strategic management.*

74. Cowan (2009), *Walking the tightrope*; Maxwell (2015), *An Exploration of Human Resource Personnel and Toxic Leadership*; Webster et al. (2014), Fight, flight or freeze.

75. Lipman-Blumen (2006), *The allure of toxic leaders.*

Printed in Great Britain
by Amazon

38106581R00129